Canadian Cookbook

From Toronto to Saskatchewan Discover Delicious Canadian Recipes from the Heart of the Maple Country

By
BookSumo Press
All rights reserved

Published by
http://www.booksumo.com

ENJOY THE RECIPES?

KEEP ON COOKING WITH 6 MORE FREE COOKBOOKS!

Visit our website and simply enter your email address to join the club and receive your 6 cookbooks.

http://booksumo.com/magnet

https://www.instagram.com/booksumopress/

https://www.facebook.com/booksumo/

LEGAL NOTES

All Rights Reserved. No Part Of This Book May Be Reproduced Or Transmitted In Any Form Or By Any Means. Photocopying, Posting Online, And / Or Digital Copying Is Strictly Prohibited Unless Written Permission Is Granted By The Book's Publishing Company. Limited Use Of The Book's Text Is Permitted For Use In Reviews Written For The Public.

Table of Contents

Raisin Tarts 9

Buttered Roasted Turkey 10

Fried Spicy Chicken 11

Prosciutto Wrapped Pesto Chicken 12

Stuffed Mushroom Caps 13

Spicy Buttered Trout 14

Cream Cheese Stuffed Mushrooms 15

Avocado & Tomato Dip 16

Hot Cheesy Chicken Dip 17

Sweet Bacon Canadian Snacks 18

Canadian Asian Rice and Beef 19

Baked Blueberry & Coconut Oatmeal 20

Buttered Garlicky Potatoes 21

Cheesy Spaghetti in Rosemary Sauce 22

Grilled Herbed Veggies 23

Brown Butter Spiced Banana Bread 24

Chilled Creamy Broccoli Salad 25

Pesto Spinach and Tomatoes 26

Roasted Cauliflower, Garlic, and Leek Soup 27

Chicken & Mushroom Kabobs with Rice 28

Shawarma 29

Buttered Apple Scones 30

Moist Egg Pancakes 31

Tangy Swordfish 32

Crème Brulee 33

French Dessert I 34

Onion Soup I 35

Swiss and Bacon Quiche 36

Burgundy Beef I 37

French Potato Bake 38

Maggie's Easy Cordon Bleu 39

Maggie's Easy Crepes I 40

Restaurant Style Onion Soup 41

Classical French Style Bread 43

Parmesan, Eggplant, and Mushroom Bake 44

Salmon with Lemon Sauce 45

Parisian Stew 46

French Dump Dinner I 47

Tapenade I 48

Gruyere 49

Tapenade II 50

Gruyere Pie 51

Artisan Mozzarella Bake of Garlic & Artichokes 52

Southern French Rice 53

Southern French Spice Mix 54

French Style Dump Dinner II 55

Restaurant Style Asparagus 56

Easy Filet Mignon 57

Homemade French Dressing 58

Classical Coq Au Vin 59

Maggie's Easier Coq Au Vin 61

Black Bean Quinoa Burgers 62

Quinoa Summer Salad 63

Quinoa in Classical Greek Style 64

Chipotle Quinoa 65

Noodles Hungarian Style 66

Comforting Noodle Soup 67

Pennsylvanian Noodles 68

Fabulous Noodles 69

Easy Homemade Noodles II 70

Spring Veggies Fiesta 71

Zesty Veggies Roast 72

Cherry Potato Roast Salad 73

Rosemary Roasted Rooty Veggies 74

White Wine Roasted Mixed Veggies Salad 75

Breakfast Pancakes 76

Apple Cinnamon Pancakes 77

Peanut Butter Chocolate Pancakes 78

Chicken Pancakes 79

True Tuscan Pancakes 80

Swiss Style Potato Soup 81

Peanut Potato Soup 82

Cream of Chicken Potato Soup 83

Cream of Mushroom Potato Soup 84

Chestnut Turkey for Christmas Eve 85

Harvest Moon Turkey 87

Apple Cider Thyme Turkey 89

Cola Turkey 90

Granny Smith Turkey 91

Simple Omelet 92

Japanese Omelet Treat 93

Spinach Omelet 94

Fort Collins Omelet 95

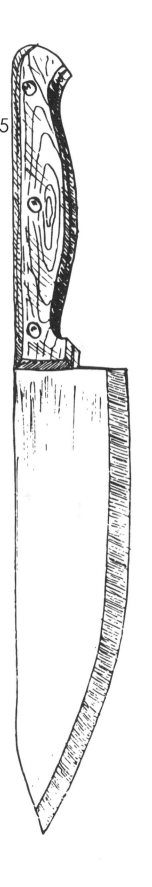

Stovetop Veggie Stew 96

Carrots and Beef Stew 97

Ranch Style Stew 98

Classical Beef Stew 99

Cottage Cheese Cinnamon Waffle 100

Chicken Nugget Waffle 101

Coconut Waffle 102

Buttermilk Greek Waffle 103

Raisin Tarts

Prep Time: 15 mins
Total Time: 35 mins

Servings per Recipe: 16
Calories   258 kcal
Fat   10 g
Carbohydrates   40.7g
Protein   2.6 g
Cholesterol   31 mg
Sodium   133 mg

Ingredients

16 (3 inch) unbaked tart shells
1 C. raisins
3/4 C. brown sugar
1/4 C. butter, softened
2 eggs
1/2 C. maple syrup
1 tbsp all-purpose flour

1 tbsp vanilla extract
pinch of salt

Directions

1. Set your oven to 350 degrees F before doing anything else.
2. Place the raisins in the bottom of the tart shells evenly and arrange the shells onto a large baking sheet.
3. In a bowl, add the butter and sugar and beat till smooth.
4. Add the remaining ingredients and beat till well combined and transfer the mixture into the tart shells so they are about 3/4 full.
5. Cook everything in the oven for about 16 minutes, turning the baking sheet once half way.

BUTTERED
Roasted Turkey

🥣 Prep Time: 30 mins
🕐 Total Time: 4 hrs 30 mins

Servings per Recipe: 24
Calories	663 kcal
Fat	33.8 g
Carbohydrates	13.7g
Protein	72.2 g
Cholesterol	1211 mg
Sodium	710 mg

Ingredients

- 1 (18 lb) whole turkey
- 1/2 C. unsalted butter, softened
- salt and freshly ground black pepper to taste
- 1 1/2 quarts turkey stock
- 8 C. prepared stuffing

Directions

1. Set your oven to 325 degrees F before doing anything else and arrange the rack in the lowest position of the oven. Now arrange a rack into a large roasting pan. Remove the neck and giblets from the turkey and then rinse and pat dry the turkey completely.
2. Arrange the turkey, breast side up over the rack in the roasting pan and stuff the body cavity with stuffing loosely.
3. Coat the skin of the turkey with the butter evenly and sprinkle with the salt and black pepper.
4. Cover the turkey with foil and place 2 C. of the broth in the roasting pan.
5. Roast for about 2 1/2 hours, basting and adding 1-2 C. of the broth after every 30 minutes.
6. Remove the foil paper and cook for 1 1/2 hours more.
7. Place the turkey onto a large cutting board for about 20-30 minutes before slicing.

Fried Spicy Chicken

Prep Time: 10 mins
Total Time: 50 mins

Servings per Recipe: 3
Calories   710 kcal
Fat   46.9 g
Carbohydrates   43.7 g
Protein   28 g
Cholesterol   136 mg
Sodium   2334 mg

Ingredients

- oil for deep frying
- 1 C. unbleached all-purpose flour
- 2 tsps salt
- 1/2 tsp ground black pepper
- 1/2 tsp cayenne pepper
- 1/4 tsp garlic powder
- 1/2 tsp paprika
- 1 egg
- 1 C. milk
- 3 skinless, boneless chicken breasts, cut into 1/2-inch strips
- 1/4 C. hot pepper sauce
- 1 tbsp butter

Directions

1. In a shallow dish, add the milk and egg and beat till well combined.
2. In another shallow dish, mix together the flour, garlic powder, paprika, cayenne pepper, salt and black pepper.
3. Dip the chicken strips in the milk mixture and then coat them with the flour mixture evenly.
4. Repeat this process for a double coating and refrigerate the strips for about 20 minutes.
5. Meanwhile in a large pan or deep fryer, heat the oil to 375 degrees F.
6. Carefully add the chicken strips into the hot oil and fry for about 5-6 minutes or till browned nicely.
7. In a microwave safe bowl, mix together the butter and hot pepper sauce and microwave on high for about 20-30 seconds or till melted.
8. Add the chicken strips and sauce into a bowl and stir to combine before serving.

PROSCIUTTO Wrapped Pesto Chicken

Prep Time: 10 mins
Total Time: 35 mins

Servings per Recipe: 4
Calories   312 kcal
Fat   19.3 g
Carbohydrates   2g
Protein   31.5 g
Cholesterol   83 mg
Sodium   434 mg

Ingredients

4 skinless, boneless chicken breast halves
1/2 C. prepared basil pesto, divided

4 thin slices prosciutto, or more if needed

Directions

1. Set your oven to 400 degrees F before doing anything else and grease a baking dish.
2. Spread the pesto over the chicken breasts evenly and then with a piece of prosciutto wrap each breast.
3. Arrange the breasts into the prepared baking dish in a single layer.
4. Cook everything in the oven for about 25 minutes or till the desired doneness.

Stuffed Mushroom Caps

Prep Time: 15 mins
Total Time: 30 mins

Servings per Recipe: 3
Calories	123 kcal
Fat	11 g
Carbohydrates	1.5g
Protein	5.1 g
Cholesterol	33 mg
Sodium	241 mg

Ingredients

- 1/4 C. butter
- 2 cloves garlic, minced
- 6 peeled and deveined large shrimp
- 6 mushrooms, stems removed
- 2 tbsps shredded mozzarella cheese

Directions

1. Set your oven to 325 degrees F before doing anything else and lightly grease a 9x5-inch baking dish.
2. In a skillet, melt the butter with garlic on medium heat and cook the shrimp for about 3 minutes.
3. In each mushroom cap, place 1 shrimp and arrange into the prepared baking dish.
4. Place the garlic butter from the skillet over the mushroom cap and top with cheese evenly.
5. Cook everything in the oven for about 10-15 minutes or till the top becomes golden brown and bubbly.

SPICY Buttered Trout

Prep Time: 20 mins
Total Time: 30 mins

Servings per Recipe: 6
Calories	420 kcal
Fat	35.3 g
Carbohydrates	1.8 g
Protein	24.3 g
Cholesterol	148 mg
Sodium	428 mg

Ingredients

- 1 tbsp paprika
- 2 tsps dry mustard
- 1 tsp cayenne pepper
- 1 tsp ground cumin
- 1 tsp black pepper
- 1 tsp white pepper
- 1 tsp dried thyme
- 1 tsp salt
- 3/4 C. unsalted butter, melted
- 6 (4 oz.) fillets trout
- 1/4 C. unsalted butter, melted

Directions

1. In a bowl, mix together the mustard, spices, thyme and salt.
2. Heat a heavy cast iron skillet on high heat for about 10 minutes.
3. In a shallow dish, place the melted butter.
4. Coat each trout fillet with the butter and sprinkle with the spice mixture evenly.
5. Add the trout fillets into the hot skillet in batches.
6. Pour 1 tsp of melted butter on each fillet and cook for about 2 minutes.
7. Flip and pour 1 tsp over each fillet and cook till desired doneness.
8. Repeat with the remaining fillets.

Cream Cheese Stuffed Mushrooms

Prep Time: 10 mins
Total Time: 30 mins

Servings per Recipe: 20
Calories	123 kcal
Fat	11 g
Carbohydrates	1.5g
Protein	5.1 g
Cholesterol	33 mg
Sodium	241 mg

Ingredients

- 1/2 C. chopped green onions
- 2 (8 oz.) packages cream cheese, softened
- 20 fresh mushrooms, stems removed
- 1 lb sliced bacon, cut in half

Directions

1. Set your oven to 350 degrees F before doing anything else.
2. In a bowl, add the cream cheese and green onion and mix till well combined.
3. Stuff the each mushroom cap with the cream cheese mixture evenly.
4. With a piece of the bacon slice, wrap the each mushroom cap and secure with toothpicks.
5. Arrange the mushroom caps into a baking sheet in a single layer and Cook everything in the oven for about 20 minutes.

AVOCADO & Tomato Dip

Prep Time: 10 mins
Total Time: 10 mins

Servings per Recipe: 4
Calories	262 kcal
Fat	22.2 g
Carbohydrates	18g
Protein	3.7 g
Cholesterol	0 mg
Sodium	596 mg

Ingredients

- 3 avocados, peeled, pitted, and mashed
- 1 lime, juiced
- 1 tsp salt
- 1/2 C. diced onion
- 3 tbsps chopped fresh cilantro
- 2 roma tomatoes, diced
- 1 tsp minced garlic
- 1 pinch ground cayenne pepper

Directions

1. In a large bowl, mix together all the ingredients.
2. Serve immediately or you can refrigerate, covered for at least 1 hour for better flavor.

Hot Cheesy Chicken Dip

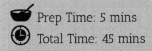
Prep Time: 5 mins
Total Time: 45 mins

Servings per Recipe: 20
Calories   284 kcal
Fat   22.6 g
Carbohydrates   8.6 g
Protein   11.1 g
Cholesterol   54 mg
Sodium   552 mg

Ingredients

- 2 (10 oz.) cans chunk chicken, drained
- 2 (8 oz.) packages cream cheese, softened
- 1 C. Ranch dressing
- 3/4 C. pepper sauce
- 1 1/2 C. shredded Cheddar cheese
- 1 bunch celery, cleaned and cut into 4 inch pieces
- 1 (8 oz.) box chicken-flavored crackers

Directions

1. In a skillet, add the chicken and hot sauce on medium heat and cook till heated completely.
2. Stir in the ranch dressing and cream cheese and cook stirring continuously till warmed and stir in half of the cheddar cheese.
3. Immediately, transfer the mixture into a slow cooker and top with the remaining cheese.
4. Set the slow cooker on Low and cook, covered for about 40 minutes or till bubbly.
5. Serve hot with the crackers and celery sticks.

SWEET BACON
Canadian Snacks

Prep Time: 10 mins
Total Time: 30 mins

Servings per Recipe: 12
Calories   356 kcal
Fat   27.2 g
Carbohydrates   18.9 g
Protein   9 g
Cholesterol   49 mg
Sodium   696 mg

Ingredients

1 lb turkey bacon
1 (16 oz.) package little smokie sausages
1 C. brown sugar, or to taste

Directions

1. Set your oven to 350 degrees F before doing anything else.
2. Cut the bacon slices into three pieces.
3. Wrap each sausage with a piece of the bacon and thread onto pre-soaked wooden skewers.
4. On a baking sheet, place the skewers in a single layer and sprinkle with brown sugar generously.
5. Cook everything in the oven till the brown sugar is melted and the bacon becomes crisp.

Canadian Asian Rice and Beef

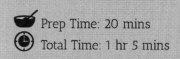

Prep Time: 20 mins
Total Time: 1 hr 5 mins

Servings per Recipe: 6
Calories	507 kcal
Fat	18.7 g
Carbohydrates	59.2g
Protein	27.4 g
Cholesterol	61 mg
Sodium	649 mg

Ingredients

- 1 1/2 lbs beef top sirloin, thinly sliced
- 1/3 C. white sugar
- 1/3 C. rice wine vinegar
- 2 tbsps frozen orange juice concentrate
- 1 tsp salt
- 1 tbsp soy sauce
- 1 C. long grain rice
- 2 C. water
- 1/4 C. cornstarch
- 2 tsps orange zest
- 3 tbsps grated fresh ginger
- 1 1/2 tbsps minced garlic
- 8 broccoli florets, lightly steamed
- 2 C. oil for frying

Directions

1. Line a large baking sheet with paper towels.
2. Arrange the beef strips onto the prepared baking sheet in a single layer and refrigerate for about 30 minutes.
3. In a small bowl, mix together sugar, orange juice concentrate, vinegar, soy sauce and salt and keep aside.
4. In a pan, mix together water and rice and bring to a boil.
5. Reduce the heat to medium-low and simmer for about 20 minutes or till tender.
6. In a skillet, heat oil on medium-high heat.
7. Coat the beef with the cornstarch evenly and cook the beef in the skillet till golden brown and crispy and transfer onto a plate.
8. Discard the fat from the skillet, leaving 1 tbsp.
9. Add the garlic, ginger and orange zest and cook till fragrant.
10. Stir in the vinegar mixture and bring to a simmer and cook for about 5 minutes or till the sauce become thick. Stir in the beef and cook till heated completely.
11. Place the rice onto serving plates and top it with the beef mixture.
12. Serve with a garnishing of broccoli.

BAKED Blueberry & Coconut Oatmeal

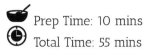

Prep Time: 10 mins
Total Time: 55 mins

Servings per Recipe: 6
Calories	422 kcal
Fat	23.7 g
Carbohydrates	45.4g
Protein	10.5 g
Cholesterol	39 mg
Sodium	397 mg

Ingredients

- 2 C. rolled oats
- 1 C. unsweetened flaked coconut
- 1/4 C. light brown sugar
- 1 tsp baking powder
- 1 tsp ground cinnamon
- 1/2 tsp salt
- 2 C. skim milk
- 1 large egg, beaten
- 3 tbsps coconut oil, softened
- 1 tsp vanilla extract
- 1 1/2 C. blueberries

Directions

1. Set your oven to 350 degrees F before doing anything else and grease an 8-inch baking dish.
2. In a large bowl, mix together coconut, oats, baking powder, brown sugar, cinnamon and salt.
3. In another bowl, add the remaining ingredients except blueberries and beat till well combined.
4. In the bottom of the prepared baking dish, place about 2/3 of the blueberries evenly.
5. Place the oat mixture over the blueberries evenly followed by the egg mixture.
6. Top everything with the remaining blueberries evenly and cook it all in the oven for about 40 minutes.
7. Remove everything from the oven and let it cool for about 5 minutes before serving.

Buttered Garlicky Potatoes

Prep Time: 10 mins
Total Time: 20 mins

Servings per Recipe: 5
Calories   330 kcal
Fat   7.2 g
Carbohydrates   62.1g
Protein   5.9 g
Cholesterol   18 mg
Sodium   178 mg

Ingredients

8 medium red potatoes, cubed
3 tbsps butter, melted
1 tbsp chopped fresh dill
2 tsps minced garlic
1/4 tsp salt

Directions

1. Arrange a steamer basket over a pan of boiling water.
2. Place the potatoes in the steamer basket and cook, covered for about 10 minutes or till the potatoes are just tender.
3. Drain the potatoes well and transfer into a bowl.
4. In a 2ndbowl, mix together remaining ingredients and transfer into the 1stbowl with the potatoes and mix well.

CHEESY Spaghetti in Rosemary Sauce

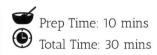

Prep Time: 10 mins
Total Time: 30 mins

Servings per Recipe: 8	
Calories	305 kcal
Fat	10.3 g
Carbohydrates	43.9 g
Protein	8.8 g
Cholesterol	26 mg
Sodium	214 mg

Ingredients

- 6 tbsps unsalted butter, divided
- 1/2 C. finely chopped onion
- 6 cloves garlic, coarsely chopped
- 1 C. chicken broth
- 2 tbsps chopped fresh rosemary
- 1 (16 oz.) package spaghetti
- 1/4 C. grated Parmesan cheese
- kosher salt and cracked black pepper to taste

Directions

1. In a large skillet, melt 1/4 C. of the butter on low heat and sauté the onion for about 10 minutes.
2. Add garlic and sauté for about 2 minutes and stir in rosemary and chicken broth.
3. Increase the heat to medium-high and cook for about 8 minutes or till the mixture reduces by 1/3.
4. Meanwhile in a large pan of lightly salted boiling water, cook the spaghetti for about 8 minutes.
5. Drain the spaghetti completely and add into the skillet and gently, stir to combine.
6. Stir in the Parmesan, remaining butter, salt and black pepper and remove from heat.
7. Serve hot with a garnishing of rosemary and extra parmesan.

Grilled Herbed Veggies

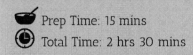

Prep Time: 15 mins
Total Time: 2 hrs 30 mins

Servings per Recipe: 6
Calories	107 kcal
Fat	4.9 g
Carbohydrates	13.3g
Protein	4.3 g
Cholesterol	0 mg
Sodium	340 mg

Ingredients

- 2 tbsps olive oil
- 2 tbsps chopped fresh parsley
- 2 tbsps chopped fresh oregano
- 2 tbsps chopped fresh basil
- 1 tbsp balsamic vinegar
- 1 tsp kosher salt
- 1/2 tsp black pepper
- 6 cloves garlic, minced
- 1 red onion, cut into wedges
- 18 spears fresh asparagus, trimmed
- 12 crimini mushrooms, stems removed
- 1 (1 lb) eggplant, sliced into 1/4 inch rounds
- 1 red bell pepper, cut into wedges
- 1 yellow bell pepper, cut into wedges

Directions

1. In a large resealable bag, add oil, vinegar, fresh herbs, garlic, salt and pepper and shake to mix.
2. Add the vegetables and tightly, seal the bag and refrigerate to marinate for about 2 hours, flipping occasionally.
3. Set your grill to high heat and grease the grill grate.
4. Cook the vegetables on the grill for about 12 minutes, flipping once half way.

BROWN BUTTER spiced Banana Bread

 Prep Time: 15 mins
Total Time: 1 hr 20 mins

Servings per Recipe: 6
Calories   389 kcal
Fat   16.8 g
Carbohydrates   55.4g
Protein   5.1 g
Cholesterol   72 mg
Sodium   439 mg

Ingredients

1/2 C. butter
3 very ripe bananas
1/4 C. brown sugar
1/4 C. white sugar
1 egg
1 tbsp vanilla extract
1 1/2 C. all-purpose flour

1 1/2 tsps baking soda
1 tsp ground cinnamon
1/2 tsp ground nutmeg

Directions

1. In a small pan, melt butter on medium heat and cook, stirring continuously for about 5-10 minutes or till browned. Remove from heat and keep aside to cool for about 15 minutes. After cooling, transfer about 1/3 C. of the butter in a bowl for use. Meanwhile, set your oven to 350 degrees F before doing anything else and grease a loaf pan.
2. In a large bowl, add the bananas and mash them completely.
3. In the bowl of bananas, add 1/3 C. of brown butter, egg, both sugars and vanilla extract and mix till well combined.
4. In another bowl, mix together flour, baking soda and spices.
5. Add the flour mixture into the banana mixture and mix till well combined.
6. Transfer the mixture onto the prepared loaf pan evenly and Cook everything in the oven for about 45 minutes or till a toothpick inserted in the center comes out clean.

Chilled Creamy Broccoli Salad

Prep Time: 25 mins
Total Time: 2 hrs 25 mins

Servings per Recipe: 6
Calories   119 kcal
Fat   3.2 g
Carbohydrates   20.1 g
Protein   4.6 g
Cholesterol   12 mg
Sodium   267 mg

Ingredients

- 3 C. broccoli florets
- 1/2 C. chopped red onion
- 1/4 C. sunflower seeds
- 1/2 C. chopped raisins
- 1/2 C. crumbled feta cheese
- 1/2 C. plain low-fat yogurt
- 1/4 C. light mayonnaise
- 2 tbsps white sugar
- 1 tbsp lemon juice
- salt and pepper to taste

Directions

1. In a large bowl, mix together broccoli, onion, raisins, sunflower seeds and feta cheese.
2. In another bowl, add the remaining ingredients and beat till well combined.
3. Add the yogurt mixture into a salad bowl and toss to coat well.
4. Refrigerate, covered for at least 2 hours.

PESTO Spinach and Tomatoes

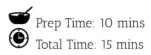

Prep Time: 10 mins
Total Time: 15 mins

Servings per Recipe: 2
Calories	272 kcal
Fat	21.8 g
Carbohydrates	15.1g
Protein	9.1 g
Cholesterol	5 mg
Sodium	267 mg

Ingredients

- 2 tbsps olive oil
- 2 garlic cloves, coarsely chopped
- 1 bunch fresh spinach, chopped
- 1 pint cherry tomatoes, halved
- 2 tbsps prepared basil pesto

Directions

1. In a large skillet, heat oil on medium heat and sauté garlic for about 1 minute.
2. Add spinach and stir fry for about 2 minutes or till wilted.
3. Stir in tomatoes and cook for about 2 minutes.
4. Stir in the pesto and serve hot.

Roasted Cauliflower, Garlic, and Leek Soup

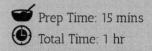

Prep Time: 15 mins
Total Time: 1 hr

Servings per Recipe: 4
Calories   292 kcal
Fat   22.5 g
Carbohydrates   19.4g
Protein   5.5 g
Cholesterol   36 mg
Sodium   1145 mg

Ingredients

- 1 head cauliflower, cut into florets
- 3 tbsps olive oil
- salt and ground black pepper to taste
- 4 cloves garlic
- 1/4 C. butter
- 2 stalks celery
- 1 leek - split, cleaned, and minced
- 1/4 C. all-purpose flour
- 4 C. chicken broth
- 1 tsp dried marjoram

Directions

1. Set your oven to 400 degrees F before doing anything else and grease a baking sheet.
2. In a bowl, add cauliflower and drizzle with oil and sprinkle with salt and black pepper.
3. Spread the cauliflower and garlic into the prepared baking sheet and Cook everything in the oven for about 15 minutes.
4. Flip the cauliflower and garlic and sauté for about 10 minutes.
5. In a large pan, melt butter on medium heat and sauté the leeks and celery for about 5 minutes or till softened.
6. Stir in the flour and cook, stirring continuously for about 2-3 minutes.
7. Add the broth, stirring continuously till well combined.
8. Stir in the cauliflower mixture and marjoram and bring to a gentle simmer and cook for about 10 minutes.
9. Remove everything from the heat and with an immersion blender, puree the soup to the desired consistency.
10. Season with salt and black pepper and serve hot.

CHICKEN & Mushroom Kabobs with Rice

Prep Time: 15 mins
Total Time: 2 hrs 45 mins

Servings per Recipe: 4	
Calories	394 kcal
Fat	4.8 g
Carbohydrates	43.7 g
Protein	41.5 g
Cholesterol	97 mg
Sodium	96 mg

Ingredients

1/2 C. light mayonnaise
1 tsp minced garlic
1/2 tsp curry powder
1/2 tsp chili powder
1/2 tsp ground ginger
1 1/2 lbs skinless, boneless chicken breast halves - cubed
1 C. uncooked white rice
2 C. water
8 oz. fresh mushrooms, sliced
1 tomato, diced
3 green onions, chopped
skewers

Directions

1. In a large bowl, mix together the mayonnaise, garlic, ginger, chili powder and curry powder.
2. Add the cubed chicken and coat it with the mixture generously and refrigerate, covered for about 2-4 hours.
3. Set your grill to medium-high heat and grease the grill grate.
4. Meanwhile in a pan, mix together the water and rice and bring to a boil.
5. Reduce the heat to low and simmer, covered for about 20 minutes or till all the liquid is absorbed.
6. Remove the chicken from the refrigerator and discard the excess marinade.
7. Thread the chicken and mushrooms onto skewers.
8. Cook on grill for about 5-10 minutes or till desired doneness, flipping occasionally.
9. Place rice onto serving plates and top them with the skewers.
10. Serve with a garnishing of tomato and onion.

Shawarma

Prep Time: 20 mins
Total Time: 45 mins

Servings per Recipe: 4
Calories   737 kcal
Fat   39.6 g
Carbohydrates   46.4 g
Protein   49.1 g
Cholesterol   114 mg
Sodium   1133 mg

Ingredients

- 1 tbsp ground coriander
- 1 tbsp ground cumin
- 1 tbsp ground cardamom
- 1 tbsp chili powder
- 1 tbsp grill seasoning
- 1 tsp smoked paprika
- 1/2 tsp ground turmeric
- 1 lemon, juiced, divided
- 1 large clove garlic, minced
- 5 tbsps extra-virgin olive oil, divided
- 4 (6 oz.) skinless, boneless chicken breast halves
- 1 large onion, sliced
- 1 red bell pepper, sliced
- 1 yellow bell pepper, sliced
- salt and ground black pepper to taste
- 1 1/2 C. Greek yogurt
- 1/4 C. tahini
- 1 tsp extra-virgin olive oil
- 4 pita bread rounds

Directions

1. Set your outdoor grill to high heat and grease the grill grate.
2. In a large bowl, add spices, garlic, 1/2 of lemon juice and 3 tbsps of oil and mix till a paste forms.
3. Add the chicken breasts and coat with paste generously.
4. Cook on the grill for about 12 minutes, flipping once half way or till desired doneness.
5. Place the chicken breasts onto a plate and let them cool and then cut into thin slices.
6. In a large skillet, heat 2 tbsps of oil on medium heat and sauté the bell peppers and onion with salt and black pepper for about 5 minutes.
7. In a bowl, mix together yogurt, tahini, remaining lemon juice, 1 tsp of oil and salt.
8. Cook the pita on grill for about 1 minute per side or till lightly charred.
9. Divide chicken and bell pepper mixture over pita breads evenly.
10. Serve with a topping of tahini yogurt.

BUTTERED Apple Scones

Prep Time: 15 mins
Total Time: 30 mins

Servings per Recipe: 12
Calories	147 kcal
Fat	4.3 g
Carbohydrates	24.6 g
Protein	2.6 g
Cholesterol	11 mg
Sodium	264 mg

Ingredients

2 C. all-purpose flour
1/4 C. white sugar
2 tsps baking powder
1/2 tsp baking soda
1/2 tsp salt
1/4 C. butter, chilled
1 apple - peeled, cored and shredded
1/2 C. milk
2 tbsps milk
2 tbsps white sugar
1/2 tsp ground cinnamon

Directions

1. Set your oven to 425 degrees F before doing anything else and grease a large baking sheet.
2. In a large bowl, mix together flour, sugar, baking soda, baking powder and salt.
3. With a pastry cutter, cut the butter into the flour mixture and mix till a crumbly mixture forms.
4. Add 1/2 C. of milk and apple and mix till a soft dough forms.
5. Place the dough onto a floured surface and gently, knead it about 8-10 times.
6. Roll the dough into 2 (6-inch) circles.
7. Arrange the circles onto the prepared baking sheet.
8. With remaining milk, brush the tops of the circles and sprinkle with the remaining sugar and cinnamon.
9. Carefully, cut each circle into 6 equal sized wedges and cook them in the oven for about 15 minutes or till golden brown.
10. Serve warm with a topping of butter.

Moist Egg Pancakes

Prep Time:	10 mins
Total Time:	20 mins

Servings per Recipe: 4
Calories   197 kcal
Fat   4.8 g
Carbohydrates   28g
Protein   9.9 g
Cholesterol   159 mg
Sodium   325 mg

Ingredients

- 1 C. all-purpose flour
- 1 tbsp baking powder
- 1 C. milk
- 3 egg yolks
- 3 egg whites

Directions

1. In a bowl, mix together flour and baking powder.
2. Add the egg yolk and milk and mix till smooth.
3. In another bowl, add the egg whites and beat till stiff peaks form.
4. Gently, fold in 1/3 of beaten egg whites and then quickly, fold in the remaining egg whites.
5. Lightly, grease a frying pan or griddle and heat on medium heat.
6. Add about 1/4 C. of mixture on the griddle and cook till golden brown from both sides.

TANGY
Swordfish

Prep Time: 10 mins
Total Time: 22 mins

Servings per Recipe: 4
Calories   258 kcal
Fat   12.3 g
Carbohydrates   5.6g
Protein   27.6 g
Cholesterol   52 mg
Sodium   708 mg

Ingredients

4 cloves garlic
1/3 C. white wine
1/4 C. lemon juice
2 tbsps soy sauce
2 tbsps olive oil
1 tbsp poultry seasoning
1/4 tsp salt
1/8 tsp pepper
4 swordfish steaks
1 tbsp chopped fresh parsley
4 slices lemon, for garnish

Directions

1. In a large glass baking dish, mix together all the ingredients except the steaks, parsley and lemon slices.
2. Add the swordfish sticks and coat it with the mixture generously and refrigerate for at least 1 hour, stirring occasionally.
3. Set your outdoor grill to high heat and grease the grill grate.
4. Cook on the grill for about 10-12 minutes, flipping once half way.
5. Serve with a garnishing of parsley and lemon wedges.

Crème Brulee

🥣 Prep Time: 10 mins
🕐 Total Time: 6 hrs 50 mins

Servings per Recipe: 4
Calories   680 kcal
Fat   55.8 g
Carbohydrates   42.6 g
Protein   6.6 g
Cholesterol   419 mg
Sodium   1155 mg

Ingredients

- 1/2 C. semi-sweet chocolate chips
- 2 C. heavy cream
- 1/4 C. white sugar
- 1 pinch salt
- 2 tsps vanilla extract
- 5 egg yolks
- 4 tbsps white sugar

Directions

1. Get a big pot of water boiling and then set your oven to 300 degrees before doing anything else.
2. Get 4 ramekin dishes and put two tbsps of chocolate pieces into each.
3. For 40 secs melt the chocolate in the microwave then stir it.
4. If the chocolate is not melted heat everything again and also stir the chocolate again.
5. Heat the following until steam forms: salt, sugar (1/4 C.), and cream.
6. Get a bowl, combine: vanilla and cream.
7. Add a ladle full of the hot sugar mix to the bowl and continue stirring. Then add some more to get the eggs hot.
8. Add everything to the ramekins equally.
9. Layer a towel in a casserole dish and then place the ramekins on top, add in the boiling water to the halfway mark of the ramekins and then cover everything in foil.
10. Cook the contents in the oven for 42 mins.
11. Then place everything in the fridge for 8 hours.
12. Add a garnishing of sugar (1 tbsp) to each, then place the dish under the broiler for 4 mins.
13. Enjoy.

FRENCH
Dessert I (Madeleines) (Lemon Cookies)

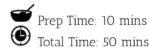

Prep Time: 10 mins
Total Time: 50 mins

Servings per Recipe: 12	
Calories	148 kcal
Fat	8.6 g
Carbohydrates	16.1g
Protein	1.9 g
Cholesterol	51 mg
Sodium	77 mg

Ingredients

2 eggs
1/2 tsp vanilla extract
1/2 tsp lemon zest
1 C. confectioners' sugar
3/4 C. all-purpose flour
1/4 tsp baking powder
1/2 C. butter, melted and cooled

Directions

1. Coat a madeleine dish with nonstick spray and then set your oven to 375 degrees before doing anything else.
2. Get a bowl, combine: lemon zest, eggs, and vanilla. Use a mixer and continue mixing for 6 mins.
3. Begin to add in the confectioners' and mix the contents for 6 more mins until everything is thick.
4. Get a 2nd bowl, combine: baking powder, and flour.
5. Add a quarter of the of the baking powder mix to the eggs and stir it in.
6. Continue in this manner until everything is combined evenly.
7. Finally add the butter and mix the contents again.
8. Fill your madeleine dish with the batter and cook it in the oven for 13 mins.
9. Let the contents cool for 2 mins then remove the cookies and top them with more sugar.
10. Enjoy.

Onion Soup I

Prep Time: 10 mins
Total Time: 50 mins

Servings per Recipe: 6
Calories	476 kcal
Fat	15.2 g
Carbohydrates	56.1g
Protein	21.8 g
Cholesterol	36 mg
Sodium	1224 mg

Ingredients

- 4 onions, chopped
- 3 tbsps butter
- 3 tbsps all-purpose flour
- 1 tsp ground black pepper
- 1 tsp white sugar
- 3 (10.5 oz.) cans beef broth
- 1 1/4 C. water
- 1/2 tsp dried parsley
- 1/4 tsp dried thyme
- 1 C. white wine
- 1 French baguette, cut into 1/2 inch slices
- 8 oz. shredded mozzarella cheese

Directions

1. Stir fry your onions in butter for 12 mins then add in: sugar, flour, and black pepper.
2. Cook and stir for 2 mins before adding in: thyme, broth, parsley, and water.
3. Let this mix gently boil for 12 mins.
4. At the same time turn on your broiler.
5. Divide the mix between the serving bowls and add a piece of bread to each with a final topping of cheese.
6. Melt the cheese under the broiler or in the oven then serve the soup.
7. Enjoy.

SWISS and Bacon Quiche

Prep Time: 30 mins
Total Time: 1 hr 5 mins

Servings per Recipe: 8
Calories   359 kcal
Fat   26.3 g
Carbohydrates   17g
Protein   13.6 g
Cholesterol   106 mg
Sodium   463 mg

Ingredients

- 1 recipe pastry for a 9 inch single crust pie
- 6 slices bacon
- 1 onion, sliced
- 3 eggs, beaten
- 1 1/2 C. milk
- 1/4 tsp salt
- 1 1/2 C. shredded Swiss cheese
- 1 tbsp all-purpose flour

Directions

1. Place some foil around a pastry shell and then set your oven to 450 degrees before doing anything else. Cook the pastry for 9 mins in the oven then take off the foil and cook the contents for 4 more mins. Then place it on the counter. Lower the heat of the oven to 325 degrees before continuing. Now stir fry your bacon, break it into pieces, and place it to the side. Stir fry the onions in the drippings, until they are soft, and remove any excess oils.
2. Get a bowl, combine: eggs, salt, milk, onions, and bacon.
3. Get a 2nd bowl, combine: flour and cheese.
4. Combine both bowls and then fill your pastry shell with the mix.
5. Cook the quiche in the oven for 37 mins.
6. Serve when then pie has cooled off considerably. Enjoy.

Burgundy Beef I

Prep Time: 20 mins
Total Time: 3 hrs 20 mins

Servings per Recipe: 4
Calories   583 kcal
Fat   31 g
Carbohydrates   21.9 g
Protein   32.2 g
Cholesterol   125 mg
Sodium   1333 mg

Ingredients

- 1/4 C. all-purpose flour
- 1 tsp salt
- 1/2 tsp ground black pepper
- 2 lbs cubed stew meat
- 4 tbsps butter
- 1 onion, chopped
- 2 carrots, chopped
- 1 clove garlic, minced
- 2 C. red wine
- 1 bay leaf
- 3 tbsps chopped fresh parsley
- 1/2 tsp dried thyme
- 1 (6 oz.) can sliced mushrooms
- 1 (16 oz.) can canned onions

Directions

1. Get a bowl, combine: pepper, salt, and flour.
2. Add in the beef, and stir the contents. Sear the beef in butter, then place everything into a baking dish. Set your oven to 350 degrees before doing anything else. Now begin to stir fry your onions, garlic, and carrots for 7 mins. Add in: the mushroom liquid, wine, thyme, bay leaf, and parsley.
3. Top the meat with this mix and cook everything in the oven for 2.5 hrs with a covering of foil. Take off the foil and add the mushrooms and canned onions.
4. Cook the meat for 35 more mins. Enjoy.

FRENCH
Potato Bake (Au Gratin)

Prep Time: 30 mins
Total Time: 2 hrs

Servings per Recipe: 4
Calories	499 kcal
Fat	25.4 g
Carbohydrates	49.3g
Protein	19.8 g
Cholesterol	77 mg
Sodium	683 mg

Ingredients

4 russet potatoes, sliced into 1/4 inch slices
1 onion, sliced into rings
salt and pepper to taste
3 tbsps butter

3 tbsps all-purpose flour
1/2 tsp salt
2 C. milk
1 1/2 C. shredded Cheddar cheese

Directions

1. Coat a baking dish with butter and then set your oven to 400 degrees before doing anything else.
2. Add half of the potatoes to the dish and then layer the onions on top.
3. Add the rest of the potatoes and top them with pepper and salt.
4. Begin to heat and stir your butter with salt and flour for 2 mins then add the milk and continue stirring and heating until it has become thick.
5. Add the cheese and continue stirring for 40 more secs until it is all melted.
6. Top the baking dish contents with the melted cheese mix and place a covering of foil over the dish.
7. Cook everything in the oven for 90 mins.
8. Enjoy after cooling for 12 mins.

Burgundy
Easy Cordon Bleu

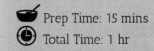

Prep Time: 15 mins
Total Time: 1 hr

Servings per Recipe: 6
Calories	584 kcal
Fat	40.9 g
Carbohydrates	7.7g
Protein	41.6 g
Cholesterol	195 mg
Sodium	655 mg

Ingredients

- 6 skinless, boneless chicken breast halves, flattened to 1/4 inch thickness
- 6 slices Swiss cheese
- 6 slices turkey ham
- 3 tbsps all-purpose flour
- 1 tsp paprika
- 6 tbsps butter
- 1/2 C. dry white wine
- 1 tsp chicken bouillon granules
- 1 tbsp cornstarch
- 1 C. heavy whipping cream

Directions

1. Get a bowl, combine: paprika and flour Layer a piece of ham and a piece of cheese on each piece of chicken then roll up the chicken and stake a toothpick through each one. Now dredge the rolls in the flour mix. Sear your chicken in hot butter then add in the bouillon and wine.
2. Place a lid on the pot, set the heat to low, and let the contents cook for 35 mins.
3. Now place the chicken to the side.
4. Get a 2nd bowl, mix: cream and cornstarch.
5. Add this to the pan which cooked the chicken and get it hot.
6. Top the chicken with the sauce. Enjoy.

MAGGIE'S
Easy Crepes I

Prep Time: 10 mins
Total Time: 30 mins

Servings per Recipe: 4	
Calories	216 kcal
Fat	9.2 g
Carbohydrates	25.5g
Protein	7.4 g
Cholesterol	111 mg
Sodium	235 mg

Ingredients

1 C. all-purpose flour
2 eggs
1/2 C. milk
1/2 C. water
1/4 tsp salt

2 tbsps butter, melted

Directions

1. Get a bowl, combine: butter, water, salt, eggs, milk, and flour.
2. Mix this liquid until it is completely smooth and combined.
3. Get your frying pan hot with oil before continuing.
4. Fry a 1/4 C. of the mix in the frying pan for 2 mins then flip the crepe and fry for 2 more mins.
5. Enjoy.

Restaurant Style Onion Soup

Prep Time: 15 mins
Total Time: 1 hr 15 mins

Servings per Recipe: 4
Calories   618 kcal
Fat   35.9 g
Carbohydrates   39.5g
Protein   29.7 g
Cholesterol   114 mg
Sodium   3433 mg

Ingredients

- 4 tbsps butter
- 1 tsp salt
- 2 large red onions, thinly sliced
- 2 large sweet onions, thinly sliced
- 1 (48 fluid oz.) can chicken broth
- 1 (14 oz.) can beef broth
- 1/2 C. red wine
- 1 tbsp Worcestershire sauce
- 2 sprigs fresh parsley
- 1 sprig fresh thyme leaves
- 1 bay leaf
- 1 tbsp balsamic vinegar
- salt and freshly ground black pepper to taste
- 4 thick slices French or Italian bread
- 8 slices Gruyere or Swiss cheese slices, room temperature
- 1/2 C. shredded Asiago
- 4 pinches paprika

Directions

1. Get some twine and tie together the following: bay leaf, thyme, and parsley.
2. Top your red and sweet onions with salt and then fry them in butter for 37 mins.
3. Try to stir the contents every 3 mins to avoid any burning.
4. Add in: Worcestershire, beef and chicken broth, and red wine. Drop the tied spices in as well.
5. Let this gently boil for 22 mins, with a low heat, and stir the mix at least 3 times. Take out the spices and add in some pepper, salt, and vinegar.
6. Place a lid on the pot and let the contents continue to stay warm with a very low level of heat.
7. Turn on the broiler and toast your bread under it for 2 mins then flip the pieces and toast for 2 more mins.
8. Grab 4 bowls and add an equal amount of soup to each.
9. Then add a piece of bread to each as well.

10. Add a topping of 2 pieces of gruyere and an equal amount of asiago to the pieces of bread and some paprika.
11. Cook the bowls under the broiler for 6 mins.
12. Enjoy.
13. NOTE: As you broil, the cheese should melt over the sides and add a touch of elegance to your dish. This is intended!

Classical
French Style Bread

🥣 Prep Time: 25 mins
🕐 Total Time: 2 hrs 40 mins

Servings per Recipe: 30
Calories   94 kcal
Fat   0.3 g
Carbohydrates   19.5g
Protein   2.9 g
Cholesterol   0 mg
Sodium   119 mg

Ingredients

6 C. all-purpose flour
2 1/2 (.25 oz.) packages active dry yeast
1 1/2 tsps salt
2 C. warm water (110 degrees F/45 degrees C)
1 tbsp cornmeal

1 egg white
1 tbsp water

Directions

1. Get bowl, mix: salt, flour (2 C.), warm water (2 C.), and yeast.
2. Use a mixer to combine the contents and then add in the rest of the flour, while continuing to stir.
3. For 12 mins knead this dough then add it to a bowl that has been coated with oil.
4. Place a covering over the bowl and let the dough rise until it has become twice its original size.
5. Now break the dough into 2 pieces and let it sit for another 12 mins.
6. Make sure you cover the dough again.
7. Shape the dough pieces into two large rectangles.
8. Place the doughs onto a baking sheet and top them with cornmeal and then brush them with 1 tbsp of water and some whisked egg whites.
9. Set your oven to 375 degrees before doing anything else.
10. Place of covering, again on the dough and let it sit for 37 mins.
11. Divide the dough in 4 pieces and cook the pieces for 22 mins in the oven.
12. Top the bread with more egg white and water
13. Continue cooking for 17 more mins.
14. Let the bread cool before serving. Enjoy.

PARMESAN, Eggplant, and Mushroom Bake (Ratatouille)

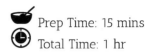

Prep Time: 15 mins
Total Time: 1 hr

Servings per Recipe: 4
Calories   251 kcal
Fat   13.5 g
Carbohydrates   24.3g
Protein   12.7 g
Cholesterol   18 mg
Sodium   327 mg

Ingredients

2 tbsps olive oil
3 cloves garlic, minced
2 tsps dried parsley
1 eggplant, cut into 1/2 inch cubes
salt to taste
1 C. grated Parmesan cheese
2 zucchini, sliced
1 large onion, sliced into rings
2 C. sliced fresh mushrooms
1 green bell pepper, sliced
2 large tomatoes, chopped

Directions

1. Grease a baking dish with half of the olive oil and then set your oven to 350 degrees before doing anything else.
2. Stir fry your garlic in the rest of the olive until seared then add in the eggplants and parsley.
3. Continue stir frying for 12 more mins. Then add some pepper and salt.
4. Layer the mix into your baking dish and top with parmesan.
5. Layer the zucchini over the parmesan and then some salt and bit more parmesan.
6. Now layer: tomatoes, onions, mushrooms, and bell peppers.
7. Add any remaining ingredients then top the entire mix with more parmesan and some salt.
8. Cook the dish for 50 mins in the oven.
9. Enjoy.

Salmon with Lemon Sauce

Prep Time: 15 mins
Total Time: 25 mins

Servings per Recipe: 2
Calories	1270 kcal
Fat	123.7 g
Carbohydrates	14.3g
Protein	38.6 g
Cholesterol	650 mg
Sodium	21153 mg

Ingredients

- 3 tbsps fresh lemon juice
- 1 tbsp olive oil
- Salt and pepper to taste
- 2 (6 oz.) skinless, boneless salmon fillets
- 3 egg yolks
- 1 tbsp hot water
- 1 C. butter, cut into small pieces
- 2 tbsps fresh lemon juice
- Salt and pepper to taste
- 2 tbsps chopped fresh chives

Directions

1. Get a saucepan and add in: salmon, lemon juice, pepper, olive oil, salt, and water (add enough to just cover the salmon).
2. Heat this mix until hot but not boiling.
3. Cook the salmon like this until the temperature of the fish is 140 degrees or it is opaque in color.
4. At the same time get some water boiling in a separate pan.
5. Begin to beat your yolks in a bowl and once the water is boiling add some of it to the yolks and continue mixing for a few mins.
6. Now place the bowl over the boiling water but it should not touching the water and continue whisking until the yolks have thickened.
7. You do not want to scramble the yolks. You are creating a sauce (hollandaise).
8. Now add a piece of butter and let it melt then add another until everything has been added to sauce.
9. Place the bowl to the side and add: pepper, salt, and lemon juice.
10. Top your cooked fish with the hollandaise and chives as well.
11. Enjoy.

PARISIAN Stew

Prep Time: 10 mins
Total Time: 1 hr 30 mins

Servings per Recipe: 8
Calories	343 kcal
Fat	20.1 g
Carbohydrates	20g
Protein	18.7 g
Cholesterol	57 mg
Sodium	491 mg

Ingredients

- 1 1/2 lbs cubed beef stew meat
- 1/4 C. all-purpose flour
- 2 tbsps vegetable oil
- 2 (14.5 oz.) cans Italian-style diced tomatoes
- 1 (14 oz.) can beef broth
- 4 carrots, chopped
- 2 potatoes, peeled and chopped
- 3/4 tsp dried thyme
- 2 tbsps Dijon-style prepared mustard
- salt and pepper to taste

Directions

1. Get a bowl, mix: flour and meat.
2. Sear the meat in veggie oil then add some pepper and salt.
3. Now add: thyme, tomatoes, potatoes, broth, and carrots.
4. Get the mix boiling.
5. Place a lid on the pot, set the heat to low, and gently boil the mix for 65 mins.
6. Add in the mustard 10 mins before the simmering is finished, stir the mix, and continue cooking for the remaining time.
7. Enjoy.

French Dump Dinner I

Prep Time: 10 mins
Total Time: 3 hrs 10 mins

Servings per Recipe: 6
Calories	484 kcal
Fat	21.1 g
Carbohydrates	35.4g
Protein	36.3 g
Cholesterol	112 mg
Sodium	1205 mg

Ingredients

- 6 skinless, boneless chicken breast halves
- 1 (10.75 oz.) can condensed cream of chicken soup
- 1 C. milk
- 4 oz. sliced ham
- 4 oz. sliced Swiss cheese
- 1 (8 oz.) package herbed dry bread stuffing mix
- 1/4 C. butter, melted

Directions

1. Get a bowl, combine: milk and chicken soup. Add this to the crock pot as well as the chicken pieces on top of the soup.
2. Add some Swiss and ham to each piece of meat and stir the contents a bit.
3. Now add the stuffing and then some butter.
4. Cook this on low for 5 hrs.
5. Enjoy.

TAPENADE I
(French Spice with Figs and Rosemary)

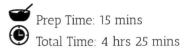

Prep Time: 15 mins
Total Time: 4 hrs 25 mins

Servings per Recipe: 6
Calories   327 kcal
Fat   24 g
Carbohydrates   26.4g
Protein   5.2 g
Cholesterol   41 mg
Sodium   361 mg

Ingredients

- 1 C. chopped dried figs
- 1/2 C. water
- 1 tbsp olive oil
- 2 tbsps balsamic vinegar
- 1 tsp dried rosemary
- 1 tsp dried thyme
- 1/4 tsp cayenne pepper
- 2/3 C. chopped kalamata olives
- 2 cloves garlic, minced
- salt and pepper to taste
- 1/3 C. chopped toasted walnuts (optional)
- 1 (8 oz.) package cream cheese

Directions

1. Boil your water and figs until the fruits are soft.
2. Once the liquid has mostly evaporated, shut the heat, and add in: pepper, cayenne, salt, olive oil, olives, thyme, garlic, balsamic, and rosemary.
3. Place the mix in the fridge for 5 hrs with a covering.
4. Top everything with cheese and nuts.
5. Serve with bread.
6. Enjoy.

Gruyere (Buttery Chicken)

Prep Time: 15 mins
Total Time: 45 mins

Servings per Recipe: 4
Calories   557 kcal
Fat   33.2 g
Carbohydrates   13.5g
Protein   46.2 g
Cholesterol   160 mg
Sodium   630 mg

Ingredients

- 1/4 C. all-purpose flour
- 1/2 tsp salt
- 1/4 tsp pepper
- 1 tsp chopped fresh parsley
- 1/2 tsp dried dill weed
- 1/4 C. butter, divided
- 4 boneless, skinless chicken breast halves
- 1 lb fresh mushrooms
- 1 onion, sliced into rings
- 1/2 C. white wine
- 8 oz. Gruyere cheese, shredded

Directions

1. Clean your pieces of chicken with fresh water and then set your oven to 350 degrees before doing anything else.
2. Get a bowl, combine: dill, flour, parsley, salt, and pepper.
3. Coat the chicken with this mix and then sear them in butter.
4. Layer the chicken pieces in a casserole dish then continue to stir fry your onions and mushrooms, until brown, in more butter.
5. Once the onions are brown, add in the wine, and let the contents boil for 4 mins.
6. Top the chicken with this mushroom mix and cook everything in the oven for 25 mins with a covering of foil.
7. Remove the foil and continue cooking for 15 more mins after adding the cheddar.
8. Enjoy.

TAPENADE II
(Olives, Garlic, and Parsley) (Bread Dip)

Prep Time: 15 mins
Total Time: 15 mins

Servings per Recipe: 8	
Calories	81 kcal
Fat	7.9 g
Carbohydrates	2.5g
Protein	0.5 g
Cholesterol	0 mg
Sodium	359 mg

Ingredients

3 cloves garlic, peeled
1 C. pitted kalamata olives
2 tbsps capers
3 tbsps chopped fresh parsley
2 tbsps lemon juice
2 tbsps olive oil
salt and pepper to taste

Directions

1. Puree the following with a blender: olive oil, garlic, lemon juice, olives, parsley, and capers.
2. Add in some pepper and salt.
3. Enjoy with toasted bread.

Gruyere Pie

🥣 Prep Time: 10 mins
🕐 Total Time: 1 hr

Servings per Recipe: 6
Calories   365 kcal
Fat   26.8 g
Carbohydrates   20.7g
Protein   11.2 g
Cholesterol   57 mg
Sodium   300 mg

Ingredients

- 1 (9 inch) refrigerated pie crust
- 2 tsps butter
- 3 leeks, chopped
- 1 pinch salt and black pepper to taste
- 1 C. light cream
- 1 1/4 C. shredded Gruyere cheese

Directions

1. Set your oven to 375 degrees before doing anything else.
2. Stir fry the leeks in butter for 12 mins then add some pepper and salt.
3. Cook the mix for 1 more min before setting the heat to low and adding the cheese and cream.
4. Get this mix hot and then add everything to the pie crust.
5. Cook the pie, for 32 mins in the oven, then let it cool for 15 mins.
6. Enjoy.

ARTISAN
Mozzarella Bake of Garlic and Artichokes

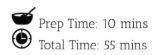

Prep Time: 10 mins
Total Time: 55 mins

Servings per Recipe: 7
Calories	365 kcal
Fat	22.7 g
Carbohydrates	24.1g
Protein	17.7 g
Cholesterol	106 mg
Sodium	774 mg

Ingredients

- 1 tbsp olive oil
- 1 clove garlic, minced
- 2 (6 oz.) cans artichoke hearts, drained
- 1/2 C. Italian seasoned bread crumbs
- 1/2 C. grated Parmesan cheese, divided
- 1 (9 inch) unbaked 9 inch pie crust
- 3 eggs, beaten
- 1 (8 oz.) package mozzarella cheese, shredded

Directions

1. Set your oven to 350 degrees before doing anything else.
2. Stir fry your garlic, until seared, then add in the artichokes, and fry the mix for 12 more mins. Now add the parmesan and the bread crumbs.
3. Get everything hot and fill the pie shell with it.
4. Top the pie with the beaten eggs and more parmesan.
5. Now add the mozzarella.
6. Cook the pie for 50 mins in the oven.
7. Enjoy.

Southern French Rice

Prep Time: 2 mins
Total Time: 25 mins

Servings per Recipe: 4
Calories   169 kcal
Fat   0.3 g
Carbohydrates   37.1g
Protein   3.3 g
Cholesterol   0 mg
Sodium   82 mg

Ingredients

- 1 C. white rice
- 2 C. chicken stock
- 1 1/2 tsps herbes de Provence
- 1 pinch sea salt
- 1 pinch pepper

Directions

1. Get the following boiling: pepper, rice, salt, stock, and herbes.
2. Once the rice is boiling, place a lid on the pot, set the heat to its lowest level, and cook for 22 mins.
3. Once the rice has cooled stir it.
4. Enjoy.
5. NOTE: See next recipe to make the spice mix.

SOUTHERN French Spice Mix (Herbes de Provence)

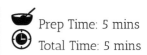

Prep Time: 5 mins
Total Time: 5 mins

Servings per Recipe: 100
Calories	2 kcal
Fat	0 g
Carbohydrates	0.3g
Protein	0.1 g
Cholesterol	0 mg
Sodium	< 1 mg

Ingredients

2 tbsps dried rosemary
1 tbsp fennel seed
2 tbsps dried savory
2 tbsps dried thyme
2 tbsps dried basil
2 tbsps dried marjoram
2 tbsps dried lavender flowers

2 tbsps dried Italian parsley
1 tbsp dried oregano
1 tbsp dried tarragon
1 tsp bay powder

Directions

1. With a mortar and pestle, combine the following: fennel seeds, bay powder, rosemary, tarragon, savory, oregano, basil, parsley, lavender, and marjoram.
2. Place the mix in a mason jar with a tight seal and store in the cupboard for continued use.
3. Enjoy.
4. NOTE: This spice mix is native to the coast of Southern France. It is best used for veggies but can be enjoyed with baked meats as well. Use this mix in all recipes which call for Herbes de Provence.

French Style Dump Dinner II (Cannellini and Kielbasa)

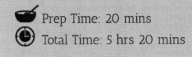

Prep Time: 20 mins
Total Time: 5 hrs 20 mins

Servings per Recipe: 6
Calories   417 kcal
Fat   9.1 g
Carbohydrates   24.9 g
Protein   51.4 g
Cholesterol   1135 mg
Sodium   1253 mg

Ingredients

2 lbs skinless, boneless chicken breast halves, cut into chunks
1 onion, quartered and thinly sliced
2 large cloves garlic, minced
1/4 C. chopped fresh parsley
1/2 tsp salt
1/4 tsp black pepper
2 (15 oz.) cans cannellini beans, drained and rinsed
1 lb turkey kielbasa, cut into 1/2-inch slices
1/3 C. dry white wine

Directions

1. Get a bowl, combine: kielbasa, onions, cannellini, parsley, pepper, and salt.
2. Layer your chicken pieces first into the crock pot. Then top with the onion mix.
3. Add in the wine and cook for 6 hrs with low heat.
4. Enjoy.

RESTAURANT STYLE
Asparagus

Prep Time: 5 mins
Total Time: 17 mins

Servings per Recipe: 4
Calories	82 kcal
Fat	6.9 g
Carbohydrates	4.4g
Protein	2.5 g
Cholesterol	0 mg
Sodium	82 mg

Ingredients

1 bunch fresh asparagus spears, trimmed
2 tbsps olive oil
1 tbsp dried Herbes de Provence
sea salt and pepper to taste

Directions

1. Cover a casserole dish with foil and then set your oven to 400 degrees before doing anything else.
2. Get a bowl, combine: pepper, asparagus, salt, olive oil, and Herbes de Provence.
3. Place the veggies into the casserole dish and cook them in the oven for 15 mins.
4. Enjoy.

Easy Filet Mignon

Prep Time: 10 mins
Total Time: 25 mins

Servings per Recipe: 4
Calories   549 kcal
Fat   46.7 g
Carbohydrates   4.9 g
Protein   27.5 g
Cholesterol   176 mg
Sodium   267 mg

Ingredients

1/4 C. coarsely crushed black peppercorns
4 (6 oz.) beef tenderloin filets, 1 1/2 inches thick
salt to taste
1 tbsp butter
1 tsp olive oil
1/3 C. beef broth
1 C. heavy cream

Directions

1. Coat the tenderloins with peppercorns and salt.
2. For 4 mins, per side, cook your steaks, in butter and olive oil.
3. Check the temperature of the meat for a 130 degree readout.
4. Then wrap the meat with some foil.
5. Add in the broth to same pan and scrape up the bottom bits.
6. Now add in the cream and cook the contents for 8 mins with a low heat until it becomes sauce like.
7. Add the tenderloins to the cream and cook for 2 more mins while flipping the meat in the sauce.
8. Serve the steaks with a liberal topping of sauce.
9. Enjoy.

HOMEMADE
French Dressing

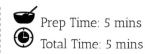

Prep Time: 5 mins
Total Time: 5 mins

Servings per Recipe: 24
Calories	73 kcal
Fat	4.6 g
Carbohydrates	8.4g
Protein	0.2 g
Cholesterol	0 mg
Sodium	80 mg

Ingredients

- 2/3 C. ketchup
- 3/4 C. white sugar
- 1/2 C. white wine vinegar
- 1/2 C. vegetable oil
- 1 small onion, quartered
- 2 tsps paprika
- 2 tsps Worcestershire sauce

Directions

1. Puree the following: Worcestershire, ketchup, paprika, sugar, onions, vinegar, and oil.
2. Once the mix is the consistency of a dressing place the contents into a mason jar with a tight seal.
3. Place the dressing in the fridge and enjoy over salad.
4. Enjoy.

Classical Coq Au Vin (Chicken & Wine with Shallots & Mushrooms)

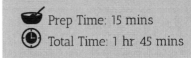

Prep Time: 15 mins
Total Time: 1 hr 45 mins

Servings per Recipe: 6
Calories   337 kcal
Fat   18 g
Carbohydrates   7.9 g
Protein   24.4 g
Cholesterol   82 mg
Sodium   582 mg

Ingredients

- 6 bone-in, skin-on chicken thighs
- 1 pinch kosher salt and freshly ground black pepper to taste
- 8 oz. bacon, sliced crosswise into 1/2-inch pieces
- 10 large button mushrooms, quartered
- 1/2 large yellow onion, diced
- 2 shallots, sliced
- 2 tsps all-purpose flour
- 2 tsps butter
- 1 1/2 C. red wine
- 6 sprigs fresh thyme
- 1 C. chicken broth

Directions

1. Set your oven to 375 degrees before doing anything else.
2. Top the chicken with some pepper and salt and begin to fry your bacon for 12 mins.
3. Now place the pieces to the side.
4. With a high heat, sear the chicken in the drippings for 5 mins per side.
5. Now remove them from the pan.
6. Stir fry your onions, shallots, and mushrooms in the drippings as well over a lower level of heat for 10 mins, then add some salt.
7. Add some butter and flour to the onions and cook the mix for 2 mins while stirring.
8. Add in the wine and get everything boiling while scraping the bottom of the pan.
9. Now add the thyme and bacon back to the boiling wine and cook the mix for 4 mins.
10. Pour in the chicken broth and place the chicken thighs into the mix in as well.
11. Get the mix gently boiling and then shut the heat.
12. Place the pan in the oven for 35 mins.
13. Now baste the chicken and cook for 30 more mins.
14. Remove the chicken from the pan and place to the side for serving.

15. Begin to heat the juices in the pan over a high heat on the stove for 6 mins and remove any fat from the sauce as it simmers.
16. Add some pepper and salt and remove the thyme.
17. Top the chicken liberally with the thick sauce.
18. Enjoy.

Maggie's Easier Coq Au Vin

Prep Time: 10 mins
Total Time: 45 mins

Servings per Recipe: 8
Calories   344 kcal
Fat   17.9 g
Carbohydrates   3.7 g
Protein   31.8 g
Cholesterol   100 mg
Sodium   498 mg

Ingredients

- 1 tbsp vegetable oil
- 1 (4 lb) whole chicken, cut into pieces
- 1 tsp salt
- 1/4 tsp ground black pepper
- 1/4 tsp garlic powder
- 1 1/2 C. red wine
- 1 1/2 C. chicken stock
- 1 onion
- 1 tbsp cornstarch
- 1/3 C. water

Directions

1. Top your chicken pieces with garlic powder, pepper, and salt.
2. Sear them in oil for 6 mins.
3. Now dip your pieces of chicken in the wine then place them back into the pan.
4. Add the following to the chicken: onions, and the rest of the wine.
5. Place a lid on the pan and cook the mix with a lower level of heat for 35 mins.
6. Get a 2nd bowl, and combine: cornstarch and water.
7. Cook this mix for 4 mins.
8. Now combine the cornstarch mix with the wine mix and stir.
9. Enjoy.

BLACK BEAN
Quinoa Burgers

Prep Time: 15 mins
Total Time: 35 mins

Servings per Recipe: 5
Calories   245 kcal
Fat   10.6 g
Carbohydrates   28.9 g
Protein   9.3 g
Cholesterol   37 mg
Sodium   679 mg

Ingredients

1 (15 oz.) can black beans, rinsed and drained
1/4 C. quinoa
1/2 C. water
1/2 C. bread crumbs
1/4 C. minced yellow bell pepper
2 tbsps minced onion
1 large clove garlic, minced
1 1/2 tsps ground cumin
1/2 tsp salt
1 tsp hot pepper sauce
1 egg
3 tbsps olive oil

Directions

1. Boil your quinoa in water. Once boiling place a lid on the pot, lower the heat, and let the mix gently cook for 17 mins.
2. Get a bowl and mash your beans. Then add in: eggs, quinoa, hot sauce, bread crumbs, salt, bell peppers, cumin, garlic, and onions.
3. Shape the quinoa mix into patties and then fry each one in olive oil for 3 mins each side.
4. Enjoy with fresh sesame seed buns.

Quinoa Summer Salad

Prep Time: 20 mins
Total Time: 30 mins

Servings per Recipe: 6
Calories	270 kcal
Fat	11.5 g
Carbohydrates	33.8g
Protein	8.9 g
Cholesterol	0 mg
Sodium	739 mg

Ingredients

- 1 C. quinoa
- 2 C. water
- 1/4 C. extra-virgin olive oil
- 2 limes, juiced
- 2 tsps ground cumin
- 1 tsp salt
- 1/2 tsp red pepper flakes, or more to taste
- 1 1/2 C. halved cherry tomatoes
- 1 (15 oz.) can black beans, drained and rinsed
- 5 green onions, finely chopped
- 1/4 C. chopped fresh cilantro
- salt and ground black pepper to taste

Directions

1. Boil your quinoa in water then place a lid on the pot, lower the heat, and let it cook for 17 mins.
2. Get a bowl, mix: red pepper, black pepper, olive oil, salt (1 tsp), cilantro, cumin, and lime juice.
3. Get a 2nd bowl, mix: onions, cooked quinoa, beans, and tomatoes.
4. Combine both bowls and toss the contents.
5. Enjoy.

QUINOA
in Classical Greek Style

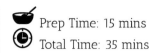

Prep Time: 15 mins
Total Time: 35 mins

Servings per Recipe: 8
Calories	278 kcal
Fat	13.9 g
Carbohydrates	20.1g
Protein	18.4 g
Cholesterol	45 mg
Sodium	713 mg

Ingredients

- 2 C. water
- 2 cubes chicken bouillon
- 1 clove garlic, smashed
- 1 C. uncooked quinoa
- 2 large cooked chicken breasts - cut into bite size pieces
- 1 large red onion, diced
- 1 large green bell pepper, diced
- 1/2 C. chopped kalamata olives
- 1/2 C. crumbled feta cheese
- 1/4 C. chopped fresh parsley
- 1/4 C. chopped fresh chives
- 1/2 tsp salt
- 2/3 C. fresh lemon juice
- 1 tbsp balsamic vinegar
- 1/4 C. olive oil

Directions

1. Boil: garlic, water, and bouillon.
2. Once boiling add the quinoa and get it boiling again.
3. Place a lid on the pot, lower the heat, and cook everything for 17 mins.
4. Remove the garlic, and place everything into a bowl.
5. Add to the quinoa: olive oil, chicken, balsamic, onions, lemon juice, bell peppers, salt, olives, chives, feta, and parsley.
6. Toss the quinoa to evenly distribute the ingredients throughout.
7. Enjoy.

Chipotle Quinoa

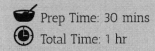

Prep Time: 30 mins
Total Time: 1 hr

Servings per Recipe: 10
Calories	233 kcal
Fat	3.5 g
Carbohydrates	42g
Protein	11.5 g
Cholesterol	0 mg
Sodium	540 mg

Ingredients

1 C. uncooked quinoa, rinsed
2 C. water
1 tbsp vegetable oil
1 onion, chopped
4 cloves garlic, chopped
1 tbsp chili powder
1 tbsp ground cumin
1 (28 oz.) can crushed tomatoes
2 (19 oz.) cans black beans, rinsed and drained
1 green bell pepper, chopped
1 red bell pepper, chopped
1 zucchini, chopped
1 jalapeno pepper, seeded and minced
1 tbsp minced chipotle peppers in adobo sauce
1 tsp dried oregano
salt and ground black pepper to taste
1 C. frozen corn
1/4 C. chopped fresh cilantro

Directions

1. Boil your quinoa in water, then place a lid on the pot, lower the heat, and let the contents gently boil for 17 mins.
2. Simultaneously, in veggie oil, stir fry your onions for 7 mins then season them with: cumin, chili powder, and garlic.
3. Cook for 2 more mins before adding: oregano, tomatoes, chipotles, black beans, jalapenos, bell peppers, and zucchini.
4. Add in your preferred amount of black pepper and salt and get the contents to a gentle boil with high then low heat.
5. Place a lid on the pot and let the contents gently cook for 22 mins.
6. Now pour in your corn and quinoa and heat for 7 more mins before shutting the heat and topping with some cilantro.
7. Enjoy.

NOODLES
Hungarian Style

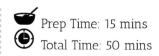
Prep Time: 15 mins
Total Time: 50 mins

Servings per Recipe: 6
Calories	414 kcal
Fat	22.6 g
Carbohydrates	35.1g
Protein	18.1 g
Cholesterol	77 mg
Sodium	809 mg

Ingredients

- 1 (8 oz.) package fine egg noodles
- 2 C. cottage cheese
- 2 C. sour cream
- 1/2 C. chopped onions
- 2 tbsp Worcestershire sauce
- 2 tbsp poppy seeds
- 1 tsp salt
- 1 tbsp grated Parmesan cheese
- 1 pinch ground paprika

Directions

1. Set your oven to 350 degrees F before doing anything else and grease a large casserole dish.
2. In a large pan of lightly salted boiling water, cook the egg noodles for about 5 minutes, stirring occasionally.
3. Drain them well and keep everything aside.
4. In a large bowl, add the noodles and remaining ingredients except the Parmesan cheese and paprika and mix well.
5. Transfer the mixture into the prepared casserole dish evenly and top with the Parmesan cheese and paprika.
6. Cook everything in the oven for about 30 minutes.

Comforting Noodle Soup

🥣 Prep Time: 10 mins
🕒 Total Time: 36 mins

Servings per Recipe: 4
Calories   536.3
Fat   12.8g
Cholesterol   115.7mg
Sodium   629.1mg
Carbohydrates   55.8g
Protein   51.1g

Ingredients

- 2 tsp olive oil or 2 tsp vegetable oil
- 2 leeks, cleaned and chopped
- 2 carrots, peeled and chopped
- 1 garlic clove, minced
- 1 stalk celery, chopped
- 3 - 4 C. cooked turkey, shredded
- 2 - 3 bay leaves
- 2 tsp dried thyme
- 1/2 tsp salt
- 1/4 tsp fresh ground black pepper
- 8 C. reduced-chicken broth
- 6 oz. egg noodles, uncooked
- 1 C. frozen green pea
- 2 tbsp fresh parsley leaves, chopped

Directions

1. In a large pan, heat the oil on medium heat, sauté the carrots, celery, leeks and garlic for about 4 minutes.
2. Stir in the turkey, thyme, bay leaves and black pepper.
3. Add the broth and bring to a boil.
4. Reduce the heat to medium-low and simmer, covered partially for about 10 minutes.
5. Uncover and again bring to a boil, then stir in the noodles.
6. Simmer for about 10 minutes.
7. Stir in the peas and simmer for about 1 minute.
8. Remove everything from the heat and discard the bay leaves.
9. Stir in the parsley and serve.

PENNSYLVANIAN
Noodles

Prep Time: 5 mins
Total Time: 15 mins

Servings per Recipe: 4
Calories 320.6
Fat 14.0g
Cholesterol 78.3mg
Sodium 113.2mg
Carbohydrates 40.6g
Protein 8.1g

Ingredients

8 oz. wide egg noodles
1/4-1/2 C. salted butter

Directions

1. In large pan of boiling water, prepare the egg noodles according to the package's directions.
2. Drain well and transfer into a large bowl.
3. Meanwhile in a small frying pan, add the butter and melt, stirring till the butter starts to become brown.
4. Pour melted butter, salt and black pepper and stir to coat well

Fabulous Noodles

Prep Time: 10 mins
Total Time: 15 mins

Servings per Recipe: 6
Calories	287.4
Fat	10.2g
Cholesterol	68.2mg
Sodium	14.0mg
Carbohydrates	40.7g
Protein	8.2g

Ingredients

kosher salt
1 (12 oz.) packages wide egg noodles
4 -6 tbsp cold unsalted butter, cut into bits
3 tbsp flat leaf parsley, chopped
fresh ground black pepper

Directions

1. In a large pan of lightly salted boiling water, cook the egg noodles for about 5 minutes, stirring occasionally.
2. Drain well, reserving 1/4 C. of the cooking liquid.
3. In a medium skillet, add the reserved hot cooking liquid on low heat.
4. Slowly, add the butter, beating continuously till a creamy sauce forms.
5. Stir in the parsley, salt and black pepper.
6. Add the noodles and toss to coat well.
7. Serve immediately.

EASY
Homemade Noodles II

Prep Time: 5 mins
Total Time: 25 mins

Servings per Recipe: 1
Calories   114.3
Fat   5.7g
Cholesterol   223.2mg
Sodium   90.3mg
Carbohydrates   7.0g
Protein   8.0g

Ingredients

6 eggs, beaten
1/2 C. water, room temperature
1/4 C. potato starch
salt

oil, for pan

Directions

1. In a bowl, mix together the potato starch and water.
2. Slowly, add the beaten eggs and salt, beating continuously till well combined.
3. Heat a lightly greased skillet on medium heat and add a thin layer of the egg mixture and cook till set.
4. Flip the side and immediately transfer onto a plate, uncooked side up.
5. Tightly roll it and cut everything into 1/4-inch circles.
6. Repeat with the remaining egg mixture.
7. These noodles can be used in any soup.

Spring Veggies Fiesta

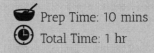

Prep Time: 10 mins
Total Time: 1 hr

Servings per Recipe: 4
Calories	193 kcal
Fat	14.1 g
Carbohydrates	15.8 g
Protein	4.3 g
Cholesterol	0 mg
Sodium	9 mg

Ingredients

- 1 eggplant, quartered and cut into 1/2-inch pieces
- 2 small yellow squash, halved lengthwise and sliced
- 1 bunch fresh asparagus, cut into 2-inch pieces
- 1 red bell pepper, seeded and cut into strips
- 1/2 red onion, sliced
- 4 cloves garlic
- 1/4 C. olive oil
- 1/4 C. red wine vinegar
- 1/4 C. chopped fresh parsley
- 2 lemons, juiced
- 3 tbsp chopped fresh oregano
- salt and freshly ground black pepper to taste

Directions

1. Before you do anything set the oven to 400 F. Coat a baking pan with some oil or cooking spray.
2. Lay in it the eggplant, yellow squash, asparagus, red bell pepper, red onion, and garlic. Cook them in the oven for 17 min.
3. Get a small bowl: Whisk in it the olive oil, vinegar, parsley, lemon juice, oregano, salt, and pepper to make the vinaigrette.
4. Drizzle the vinaigrette over the veggies then serve it.
5. Enjoy.

ZESTY
Veggies Roast

 Prep Time: 45 mins
Total Time: 2 hrs 15 mins

Servings per Recipe: 8
Calories	297 kcal
Fat	4.2 g
Carbohydrates	64.7g
Protein	6 g
Cholesterol	0 mg
Sodium	103 mg

Ingredients

- 1 large butternut squash - peeled, seeded, and cut into 1-inch pieces
- 1 large delicata squash - peeled, seeded, and cut into 1-inch pieces
- 3 sweet potatoes, peeled and cut into 1-inch pieces
- 1 (2 lb) rutabaga, peeled and cut into 1-inch pieces
- 2 red potatoes, peeled and cut into 1-inch pieces
- 2 carrots, sliced
- 1 large onion, sliced
- 2 tbsp dried rosemary
- 2 tbsp dried thyme
- 1 tsp dried oregano
- 2 tbsp extra-virgin olive oil
- 6 dried bay leaves
- 1 dash lemon juice
- 1 dash red wine vinegar
- 1 pinch salt
- 1 pinch ground black pepper

Directions

1. Before you do anything set the oven to 400 F. Coat a roasting dish with some oil or cooking spray.
2. Get a large bowl: Toss the butternut squash, delicata squash, sweet potato, rutabaga, and red potato pieces, carrots, and onion.
3. Get a small bowl: Stir in it the thyme with oregano and rosemary. Toss the veggies with the herbs mix and olive oil. Spread the veggies in the roasting dish.
4. Top them with vinegar, lemon juice and bay leaves, a pinch of salt and pepper. Cook the veggies in the oven for 1 h 32 min while stirring them 3 time. Serve your veggies warm.
5. Enjoy.

Cherry Potato Roast Salad

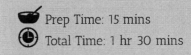
Prep Time: 15 mins
Total Time: 1 hr 30 mins

Servings per Recipe: 6
Calories   289 kcal
Fat   9.1 g
Carbohydrates   47.3g
Protein   8.6 g
Cholesterol   0 mg
Sodium   58 mg

Ingredients

- 12 new potatoes, halved
- 2 large red onions, each cut into 8 wedges
- 2 large yellow bell peppers, seeded and cubed
- 4 cloves garlic, peeled
- 1 eggplant, thickly sliced (optional)
- 1 tsp chopped fresh rosemary
- 2 tsps chopped fresh thyme
- 2 tbsp olive oil
- salt to taste
- 1 pint cherry tomatoes, halved
- 1/3 C. toasted pine nuts
- 1 (10 oz) bag baby spinach leaves
- 2 tbsp balsamic vinegar

Directions

1. Before you do anything set the oven to 400 F. Cover a baking pan with a large piece of foil.
2. Lay the potato in a ovenproof plate and microwave it for 5 min until it becomes soft.
3. Get a large bowl: Toss the cooked potato with onion, bell pepper, garlic, and eggplant, rosemary, thyme, and olive oil, a pinch of salt and pepper.
4. Transfer the veggies mix to the baking pan. Cook them in the oven for 37 min. Add the cherry tomatoes and cook them for 17 min.
5. Get a large bowl: Add the roasted veggies with spinach, vinegar and pine nuts. Stir them well and serve them.
6. Enjoy.

ROSEMARY
Roasted Rooty Veggies

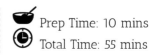

Prep Time: 10 mins
Total Time: 55 mins

Servings per Recipe: 14
Calories   135 kcal
Fat   2.6 g
Carbohydrates   27.4g
Protein   2.8 g
Cholesterol   0 mg
Sodium   116 mg

Ingredients

parsnips, peeled
6 large carrots, peeled
1 celery root, peeled
1 rutabaga, peeled
1 yellow onion, peeled
3 tbsp minced garlic

3 tbsp dried rosemary
2 tbsp extra-virgin olive oil
sea salt and freshly ground black pepper to taste

Directions

1. Before you do anything set the oven to 400 F.
2. Finely chop the veggies into 1 inch pieces. Transfer them to a large zip lock bag with garlic, rosemary, olive oil, salt, and pepper.
3. Shake the bag to coat the veggies with herbs. Spread them on a lined up baking pan. Cook them in the oven for 47 min. Serve your roasted veggies warm.
4. Enjoy.

White Wine Roasted Mixed Veggies Salad

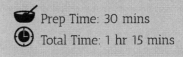

Prep Time: 30 mins
Total Time: 1 hr 15 mins

Servings per Recipe: 6
Calories   143 kcal
Fat   4.9 g
Carbohydrates   20.8g
Protein   2.8 g
Cholesterol   0 mg
Sodium   95 mg

Ingredients

1 C. diced, raw beet
4 carrots, diced
1 onion, diced
2 C. diced potatoes
4 cloves garlic, minced
1/4 C. canned garbanzo beans (chickpeas), drained
2 tbsp olive oil
1 tbsp dried thyme leaves
salt and pepper to taste
1/3 C. dry white wine
1 C. torn beet greens

Directions

1. Before you do anything set the oven to 400 F. Grease a casserole dish.
2. Toss in it the beet, carrot, onion, potatoes, garlic, and garbanzo beans. Add the olive oil with thyme, a pinch of salt and pepper. Stir them well.
3. Cook the veggies in the oven for 32 while stirring them halfway through time. Add the wine and stir it. Cook the veggies again for 17 min.
4. Adjust the seasoning of your roasted veggies then serve them warm.
5. Enjoy.

BREAKFAST
Pancakes

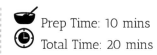

Prep Time: 10 mins
Total Time: 20 mins

Servings per Recipe: 4
Calories	304 kcal
Fat	2.7 g
Carbohydrates	64.6g
Protein	9.6 g
Cholesterol	0 mg
Sodium	734 mg

Ingredients

- 2 C. white whole wheat flour
- 2 tbsp baking powder
- 2 tbsp ground flax meal
- 17 fluid oz. orange juice
- 1 tsp orange extract

Directions

1. In a bowl, mix together the flour, baking powder and flax meal.
2. Add the orange juice and orange extract into flour mixture and mix till well-combined.
3. Heat a lightly greased griddle on medium-high heat.
4. Add the mixture by large spoonfuls into the griddle and cook for about 3-4 minutes.
5. Flip and cook for about 2-3 minutes.
6. Repeat with the remaining mixture.

Apple Cinnamon Pancakes

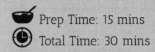

Prep Time: 15 mins
Total Time: 30 mins

Servings per Recipe: 2
Calories	654 kcal
Fat	28.4 g
Carbohydrates	86g
Protein	16.6 g
Cholesterol	421 mg
Sodium	525 mg

Ingredients

- 3 tbsp butter
- 1 large apple, cored and sliced
- 1/2 C. white sugar, divided
- 2 tsp ground cinnamon
- 4 eggs
- 1/3 C. milk
- 1/3 C. all-purpose flour
- 1 tsp baking powder
- 1 tsp vanilla extract
- 1 pinch salt

Directions

1. Set your oven to 400 degrees F before doing anything else.
2. In an oven proof skillet, melt the butter on medium heat.
3. Add the apple slices, 1/4 C. of the sugar and cinnamon and cook, stirring for about 5 minutes.
4. Meanwhile in a large bowl, add the eggs, milk, flour, remaining 1/4 C. of the sugar, baking powder, vanilla extract and salt and beat till smooth.
5. Place the mixture over the apple slices evenly.
6. Cook in the oven for about 10 minutes.
7. Remove from the oven and run a spatula around the edges of the pancake to loosen.
8. Invert the skillet over a large plate and serve.

PEANUT BUTTER Chocolate Pancakes

 Prep Time: 15 mins
Total Time: 40 mins

Servings per Recipe: 4
Calories   484 kcal
Fat   23.4 g
Carbohydrates   58.2g
Protein   13.5 g
Cholesterol   77 mg
Sodium   737 mg

Ingredients

1 1/4 C. all-purpose flour
1 tbsp baking powder
1/2 tsp salt
2 tbsp brown sugar
1 1/2 C. milk
1 egg, beaten

3 tbsp butter, melted
1 tsp vanilla extract
1/4 C. peanut butter
1/4 C. chocolate chips
1 ripe banana, diced

Directions

1. In a bowl, mix together the flour, baking powder, salt and brown sugar.
2. In another bowl, add the egg and milk and beat till well combined.
3. Add the peanut butter and stir till smooth.
4. Add the milk mixture into the flour mixture and mix till just moistened.
5. Add the melted butter and vanilla extract and beat to combine.
6. Gently fold in the chocolate chips and diced banana.
7. Heat a large nonstick skillet on medium heat.
8. Add about 1/4 C. of the mixture into the skillet and cook for about 2 minutes.
9. Flip and cook for about 2-3 minutes.
10. Repeat with the remaining mixture.

Chicken Pancakes

Prep Time: 6 mins
Total Time: 21 mins

Servings per Recipe: 4
Calories	321 kcal
Fat	17.8 g
Carbohydrates	9.6 g
Protein	29.1 g
Cholesterol	116 mg
Sodium	441 mg

Ingredients

- 1 lb. skinless, boneless chicken breast meat - finely chopped
- 1/2 medium onion, finely chopped
- 3 tbsp mayonnaise
- 1 egg, lightly beaten
- 1/3 C. all-purpose flour
- salt and pepper to taste
- 2 tbsp vegetable oil

Directions

1. In a large bowl, add the chicken, onion, mayonnaise, egg, flour, salt and pepper and mix till well combined.
2. In a skillet, heat the oil on medium heat.
3. Add about 1/4 C. of the chicken mixture into the skillet and cook till browned from both sides.
4. Repeat with the remaining mixture.
5. Serve hot.

TRUE
Tuscan Pancakes

Prep Time: 5 mins
Total Time: 20 mins

Servings per Recipe: 4
Calories 350 kcal
Fat 24.9 g
Carbohydrates 15g
Protein 16.7 g
Cholesterol 61 mg
Sodium 681 mg

Ingredients

3/4 C. baking mix (such as Bisquick (R))
1 (8 oz.) package Cheddar cheese, shredded
1/3 C. water
5 tsp prepared pesto, see appendix

Directions

1. Heat a greased griddle.
2. In a bowl, add the baking mix, water, Cheddar cheese and pesto and mix till well combined.
3. Add about 1/4 C. of the mixture into the griddle and cook for about 2-3 minutes per side.
4. Repeat with the remaining mixture.

Swiss Style Potato Soup

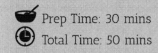

Prep Time: 30 mins
Total Time: 50 mins

Servings per Recipe: 6
Calories	311 kcal
Fat	13.1 g
Carbohydrates	37.1g
Protein	12.1 g
Cholesterol	40 mg
Sodium	638 mg

Ingredients

- 4 potatoes, peeled and quartered
- 1 small carrot, finely chopped
- 1/2 stalk celery, finely chopped
- 1 small onion, minced
- 1 1/2 C. vegetable broth
- 1 tsp salt
- 2 1/2 C. milk
- 3 tbsp butter, melted
- 3 tbsp all-purpose flour
- 1 tbsp dried parsley
- 1 tsp ground black pepper
- 1 C. shredded Swiss cheese

Directions

1. In a large pan, add the potatoes, carrots, celery, onion, vegetable broth and salt and bring to a boil.
2. Reduce the heat and simmer, covered till the potatoes become just tender.
3. With a potato masher, mash the mixture slightly and stir in the milk.
4. In a small bowl, add the butter, flour, parsley and pepper and beat to combine.
5. Add the butter mixture into the potato mixture.
6. Cook and stir on the medium heat till the mixture becomes thick and bubbly.
7. Remove from the heat and immediately, stir in the cheese and stir till the cheese is almost melted.
8. Keep aside the soup for about 5 minutes.

PEANUT
Potato Soup

 Prep Time: 30 mins
Total Time: 50 mins

Servings per Recipe: 8
Calories	207 kcal
Fat	9 g
Carbohydrates	28.7g
Protein	5 g
Cholesterol	11 mg
Sodium	462 mg

Ingredients

- 1/2 C. sour cream
- 1 tsp grated lime zest
- 2 large sweet potatoes, peeled and cubed
- 1 tbsp butter
- 1 onion, sliced
- 2 cloves garlic, sliced
- 4 C. chicken stock
- 1/2 tsp ground cumin
- 1/4 tsp crushed red pepper flakes
- 2 tbsp grated fresh ginger root
- 1/4 C. smooth peanut butter
- 1 lime, juiced
- 2 tbsp chopped fresh cilantro
- salt to taste
- 1 large roma (plum) tomato, seeded and diced

Directions

1. In a small bowl, mix together the sour cream and lime zest and refrigerate to allow the flavors to blend.
2. In a large pan, melt the butter on medium heat and sauté the onion and garlic for about 5 minutes.
3. Add the sweet potatoes, chicken broth, cumin, chili flakes and ginger and bring to a boil.
4. Reduce the heat to low, and simmer, covered for about 15 minutes.
5. With an immersion blender, puree the soup.
6. Add the peanut butter into the soup, beating continuously till well combined.
7. Simmer till heated completely.
8. Stir in the lime juice and salt.
9. Place the soup into the warm bowls and top with a dollop of the reserved sour cream, a few pieces of the diced tomato and a sprinkle of the cilantro.

Cream of Chicken Potato Soup

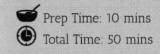 Prep Time: 10 mins
Total Time: 50 mins

Servings per Recipe: 6
Calories	404 kcal
Fat	24.8 g
Carbohydrates	32.9 g
Protein	12.5 g
Cholesterol	42 mg
Sodium	1026 mg

Ingredients

- 8 slices bacon, optional
- 1 C. chopped onion
- 4 C. cubed potatoes
- 2 (10.75 oz.) cans condensed cream of chicken soup
- 2 1/2 C. milk
- salt to taste
- ground black pepper to taste
- 1 tsp dried dill weed

Directions

1. Heat a large pan and cook the bacon till browned completely.
2. Transfer the bacon onto a paper towel lined plate to drain and then crumble it.
3. Discard the bacon grease, leaving about 3 tbsp inside the pan.
4. Heat the bacon grease on medium heat and cook the onion till browned.
5. Add the potatoes and enough water to cover.
6. Cook, covered for about 15-20 minutes.
7. In a bowl, add the cream of chicken soup and milk and mix till smooth.
8. Add the milk mixture into the soup mixture and cool till just heated.
9. Stir in the salt, pepper and dill weed and remove from the heat.
10. Serve the soup with a topping of the bacon.

CREAM of Mushroom Potato Soup

Prep Time: 30 mins
Total Time: 50 mins

Servings per Recipe: 9
Calories   642 kcal
Fat   38.9 g
Carbohydrates   41.2g
Protein   31.8 g
Cholesterol   105 mg
Sodium   2352 mg

Ingredients

8 unpeeled potatoes, cubed
1 onion, chopped
2 stalks celery, diced
6 cubes chicken bouillon
1 pint half-and-half cream
1 lb. bacon - cooked and crumbled, optional

1 (10.75 oz.) can condensed cream of mushroom soup
2 C. shredded Cheddar cheese

Directions

1. In a large soup pan mix together the potatoes, onions, celery, bouillon cubes and enough water to cover the all ingredients and bring to a boil on medium heat.
2. Simmer for about 15 minutes.
3. Add the half and half, bacon and cream of mushroom soup and stir till smooth and creamy.
4. Add the cheese and stir till melts completely.
5. Simmer on low heat till the potatoes are cooked through.

Chestnut Turkey for Christmas Eve

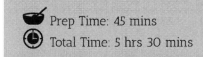

Prep Time: 45 mins
Total Time: 5 hrs 30 mins

Servings per Recipe: 6
Calories	942 kcal
Fat	70.1 g
Carbohydrates	4.6 g
Protein	68.7 g
Cholesterol	256 mg
Sodium	974 mg

Ingredients

- 2 lb. chestnuts
- 2 C. butter
- 2 C. minced onion
- 2 C. minced celery
- 10 C. dried bread crumbs
- 1 tsp dried thyme
- 1 tsp dried marjoram
- 1 tsp dried savory
- 1 tsp dried rosemary
- 12 lb. whole turkey, neck and giblets removed
- salt and freshly ground black pepper to taste

Directions

1. With a sharp knife, cut a cross on the flat side of each chestnut.
2. In a pan of the water, simmer the chestnuts, covered for about 5 minutes.
3. Drain well.
4. Remove the shells and inner brown skins from the hot chestnuts.
5. In the same pan, add the fresh water and cook the chestnuts for about 20-30 minutes.
6. Drain the chestnuts and then chop roughly.
7. For the stuffing in a medium pan, melt the butter on medium heat and sauté the onions and celery till tender.
8. Add the bread crumbs, chestnuts, thyme, marjoram, savory and rosemary and stir to combine well.
9. Remove from the heat.
10. Set your oven to 350 degrees F and arrange a rack in a large roasting pan.
11. Rinse the turkey under the running cold water and with the paper towels, pat dry.
12. Rub the salt and pepper in the turkey cavities.
13. Stuff the turkey cavities with the chestnut stuffing loosely.
14. With the skewers, close the skin and tie drumsticks together.
15. Arrange the turkey onto the rack in the roasting pan.

16. Cook in the oven for about 3 1/2 - 4 1/2 hours.
17. Cover the turkey with a piece of the foil loosely during the last half of roasting time to avoid the over browning.
18. Remove from the oven and transfer onto platter for about 20 minutes before carving.

Harvest Moon Turkey

Prep Time: 30 mins
Total Time: 8 hrs 10 mins

Servings per Recipe: 15
Calories	1019 kcal
Fat	53.7 g
Carbohydrates	7.3g
Protein	111.3 g
Cholesterol	363 mg
Sodium	410 mg

Ingredients

- 1 (18 lb.) whole turkey, thawed
- 1 1/4 C. chilled butter, diced
- 1 lb. baby carrots
- 2 large onions, roughly chopped
- 3 stalks celery, roughly chopped
- 1 whole head garlic, cut in half crosswise
- 3 tbsp chopped fresh thyme
- 3 tbsp chopped fresh sage
- 2 bay leaves
- 1 (750 milliliter) bottle chilled Chardonnay wine, optional
- salt and ground black pepper to taste

Directions

1. Set your oven to 350 degrees F before doing anything else and arrange a rack in a roasting pan.
2. Remove the neck and giblets from the inside of the turkey.
3. Rinse the turkey under the running cold water and with the paper towels, pat dry.
4. Arrange the turkey onto the rack in the roasting pan.
5. With your fingers carefully, loosen the skin over the breast.
6. Place the butter cubes underneath the skin of the breast evenly.
7. Poke 4-5 wooden toothpicks through the skin into the meat to secure the skin.
8. In a bowl, mix together the carrots, onions, celery, 2 garlic head halves, thyme, sage, bay leaves, salt and black pepper.
9. Stuff the turkey cavity with the vegetables and place the remaining in the bottom of the roasting pan.
10. Lift the turkey upright so the cavity opening is uppermost, and place the whole bottle of Chardonnay into the bird so that the wine flows into the pan.
11. Arrange the turkey onto the rack in the roasting pan.

12. With a piece of the foil, cover the turkey loosely.
13. Cook in the oven for about 7 hours.
14. Remove the foil and cook in the oven for about 25-30 minutes.
15. Remove from the oven and keep aside for about 10 minutes before carving.
16. Serve cooked carrots, onion, and celery alongside the turkey.

Apple Cider Thyme Turkey

Prep Time: 25 mins
Total Time: 1 hr 40 mins

Servings per Recipe: 15
Calories   952 kcal
Fat   37.7 g
Carbohydrates   48.6 g
Protein   98.1 g
Cholesterol   286 mg
Sodium   9387 mg

Ingredients

- 1 (16 lb.) whole turkey, neck and giblets removed
- 1 1/2 gallons water
- 1 gallon apple cider
- 1 1/2 C. kosher salt
- 1 C. white sugar
- 1/4 C. extra-virgin olive oil
- 1/4 tsp dried thyme
- 1/4 tsp poultry seasoning

Directions

1. Rinse the turkey under the running cold water.
2. In a large pan, add the water, apple cider, kosher salt and sugar and stir till the salt and sugar are dissolved completely.
3. Submerge the turkey in the brine refrigerate, covered for about 8 hours or overnight.
4. Set your oven to 325 degrees F.
5. Remove turkey from brine.
6. Rinse the turkey under the running cold water and with the paper towels, pat dry.
7. Arrange the turkey in a large roasting pan, breast side up.
8. With your fingers carefully, loosen the skin over the turkey breast and thighs.
9. In a small bowl, mix together the olive oil, thyme and poultry seasoning.
10. Rub the seasoned oil over the turkey and underneath the loosened skin evenly.
11. With a piece of the foil, cover the turkey loosely.
12. Cook in the oven for about 3 1/4-3 3/4 hours.
13. Remove the foil and cook in the oven for about 45 minutes.
14. Transfer the turkey into a platter for about 30 45 minutes before carving.

COLA Turkey

Prep Time: 10 mins
Total Time: 4 hrs 25 mins

Servings per Recipe: 12
Calories	993 kcal
Fat	50.1 g
Carbohydrates	4.6g
Protein	122.6 g
Cholesterol	378 mg
Sodium	385 mg

Ingredients

- 1 (16 lb.) whole turkey - thawed, neck and giblets removed
- 2 C. cola-flavored carbonated beverage (such as Coke(R))
- 1/2 C. butter, softened
- salt and ground black pepper to taste

Directions

1. Set your oven to 325 degrees F before doing anything else.
2. Rinse the turkey under the running cold water and with the paper towels, pat dry.
3. With your hands, spread the butter over the whole turkey evenly.
4. Arrange the turkey into a large roasting pan.
5. Place the cola over the turkey and sprinkle with the salt and black pepper evenly.
6. Cook in the oven for about 4-5 hours, basting with the pan drippings after every 30 minutes.
7. Remove from the oven and cover with a piece of the foil loosely for about 10-5 minutes before carving.

Granny Smith Turkey

Prep Time: 20 mins
Total Time: 4 hrs 30 mins

Servings per Recipe: 12
Calories	774 kcal
Fat	40.3 g
Carbohydrates	6.1g
Protein	91.3 g
Cholesterol	285 mg
Sodium	305 mg

Ingredients

- 1/2 C. cold butter
- 1 (12 lb.) whole turkey, neck and giblets removed
- 1 tbsp vegetable oil
- 2 Granny Smith apples - cored, peeled, and cut into 8 wedges each
- 1 large onion, cut into 8 wedges
- 1/2 whole head garlic, separated into cloves and peeled
- 1 lb. celery, cut into 2-inch lengths
- 1 tbsp poultry seasoning

Directions

1. Set your oven to 325 degrees F before doing anything else and arrange a rack in a large roasting pan.
2. Cut the butter into small pieces and refrigerate till using.
3. With your fingers, loosen the skin over the turkey breast and thighs.
4. Cut a hole in the turkey skin between the tail and body.
5. Cut another holes on each side of the turkey beneath each wing.
6. Rub the turkey skin with the vegetable oil evenly.
7. In a large bowl, add the apple, onion wedges, garlic cloves, celery and poultry seasoning and toss to coat.
8. Stuff the body and neck cavities of the turkey with the apple mixture.
9. Insert each wing tip in the hole under the wing to secure the wings.
10. Insert both legs in the hole near tail to secure the legs.
11. Arrange the turkey onto the rack in the roasting pan.
12. Insert the cold butter pieces under the loosened skin evenly.
13. Cook in the oven for about 3-3 1/2 hours.
14. Remove from the oven and cover with a piece of the foil loosely for about 40 minutes before carving.

SIMPLE Omelet

Prep Time: 10 mins
Total Time: 20 mins

Servings per Recipe: 4
Calories	128 kcal
Fat	0.1 g
Carbohydrates	0.8g
Protein	24.9 g
Cholesterol	0 mg
Sodium	371 mg

Ingredients

cooking spray
2 tbsp chopped onion
2 tbsp chopped green bell pepper
2 tbsp chopped mushrooms
salt and ground black pepper to taste

1 (32 oz.) container refrigerated pasteurized egg white substitute

Directions

1. Grease a 9x5-inch microwave-safe loaf pan with the cooking spray.
2. In the prepared loaf pan, mix together the bell pepper, mushrooms, onion, salt and black pepper. and top with the egg whites.
3. Microwave on High for about 3 minutes.
4. Remove from the microwave and stir the cooked egg white into the mushroom mixture.
5. Microwave on High for about 3 minutes.

Japanese Omelet Treat

Prep Time: 25 mins
Total Time: 35 mins

Servings per Recipe: 1
Calories	421 kcal
Fat	19.5 g
Carbohydrates	42.5g
Protein	20.9 g
Cholesterol	395 mg
Sodium	661 mg

Ingredients

1 1/2 tsp butter
1 small tomato, sliced
1/2 red bell pepper, sliced
1/4 onion, sliced
1/4 zucchini, sliced
1 oz. sliced mushrooms
1/2 C. warm cooked rice
1 tbsp ketchup
1 slice cooked bacon, chopped
1/2 tsp paprika
salt and ground black pepper to taste
2 eggs, lightly beaten

Directions

1. In a skillet, melt the butter on medium heat and cook the mushroom, zucchini, bell pepper, tomato and onion for about 5 minutes.
2. Stir in the bacon, rice, ketchup, paprika, salt and black pepper and transfer the mixture into serving plate.
3. Heat a nonstick skillet on medium heat and add the eggs in a thin layer.
4. Cook for about 5 minutes.
5. Serve the rice mixture with a topping of the omelet.

SPINACH Omelet

Prep Time: 15 mins
Total Time: 25 mins

Servings per Recipe: 2
Calories	363 kcal
Fat	26.9 g
Carbohydrates	6.3g
Protein	24.6 g
Cholesterol	425 mg
Sodium	839 mg

Ingredients

4 eggs
1 tbsp whole milk
4 pinches ground black pepper
2 pinches garlic salt
2 tsp olive oil
4 cremini mushrooms, sliced
2 tbsp chopped red onion

1 C. baby spinach, coarsely chopped
1/2 oz. crumbled Stilton cheese
1/2 C. shredded part-skim mozzarella cheese

Directions

1. In a bowl, add the milk, eggs, 4 pinches of the black pepper and 2 pinches of the garlic salt and beat well.
2. In a non-stick skillet, heat the oil on medium heat and cook the mushrooms and onion for about 5 minutes.
3. Spread the mushrooms and onion in the bottom of the skillet in an even layer and top with the spinach and egg mixture.
4. Cook for about 35 minutes.
5. Sprinkle the omelet with both cheeses and cook till cheese melts.
6. Fold the omelet in half and serve.

Fort Collins Omelet

Prep Time: 15 mins
Total Time: 30 mins

Servings per Recipe: 2
Calories	402 kcal
Fat	29.2 g
Carbohydrates	7 g
Protein	28.7 g
Cholesterol	418 mg
Sodium	1212 mg

Ingredients

- 1 slice bacon
- 3 eggs
- 1/4 C. milk
- 2 tsp vegetable oil
- 1/2 large tomato, diced
- 2 thin slices tomato, halved
- 5 oz. thinly sliced deli turkey
- 1/4 C. shredded Monterey Jack cheese
- 1/4 C. prepared hollandaise sauce
- 1 pinch dried parsley

Directions

1. Heat a large, deep skillet on medium-high heat and cook the bacon till browned completely.
2. Transfer the bacon onto a paper towel lined plate to drain and then crumble it.
3. Set the broiler of your oven and arrange oven rack about 6-inch from the heating element.
4. In a bowl, add the eggs and milk and beat till smooth.
5. In a skillet, heat the vegetable oil on medium heat.
6. Add the egg mixture and swirl the pan to coat the bottom of the skillet evenly.
7. Cook for about 1-2 minutes.
8. Gently flip the omelet over and cook for about 1 minute.
9. Transfer the omelet onto a broiler-safe baking sheet and top with the crumbled bacon, followed by the diced tomato, turkey and Monterey Jack cheese.
10. Fold the omelet in half to enclose the fillings and cook under the broiler for about 2 minutes.
11. Serve with a topping of the tomato slices, hollandaise sauce and parsley flakes.

STOVETOP
Veggie Stew

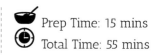

Prep Time: 15 mins
Total Time: 55 mins

Servings per Recipe: 4
Calories   200 kcal
Fat   11.9 g
Carbohydrates   23.1g
Protein   4.4 g
Cholesterol   31 mg
Sodium   331 mg

Ingredients

- 1/4 C. butter
- 2 onions, diced
- 1 stalk celery, diced
- 1 medium head cabbage, cut into squares
- 2 cloves garlic, diced
- 1 (14.5 oz.) can stewed tomatoes, with liquid
- salt and pepper to taste

Directions

1. Stir fry your garlic, celery, and onions for 7 mins in butter then add in the cabbage and cook everything for 17 more mins, with a low level of heat.
2. Stir the mix then add in some pepper, salt, and the tomatoes.
3. Place a lid on the pot and let the mix cook for 35 mins.
4. Enjoy.

Carrots and Beef Stew

Prep Time: 20 mins
Total Time: 1 hr

Servings per Recipe: 5
Calories   325 kcal
Fat   9.4 g
Carbohydrates   48.1 g
Protein   13.4 g
Cholesterol   70 mg
Sodium   960 mg

Ingredients

- 50 baby carrots, cut in half lengthwise
- 4 russet potatoes, cut into bite-sized pieces
- 1 small yellow onion, diced
- 3 stalks celery, diced
- 4 cubes beef bouillon
- 2 (8 oz.) cans oysters
- 1 tsp ground black pepper
- 1 (5 oz.) can evaporated milk
- 2 tbsps butter
- salt and pepper to taste

Directions

1. Get a big pot, add in: bouillon, carrots, celery, potatoes, and onions. Submerge the veggies in water then set the heat to a high level.
2. Get everything boiling and let the mix cook for 40 mins.
3. Now stir in the oysters and juice plus 1 tsp of pepper.
4. Continue cooking everything for 5 more mins then set the heat to a low level.
5. Add the butter and milk and combine everything smoothly then add some more pepper and salt.
6. Enjoy.

RANCH STYLE
Stew

Prep Time: 15 mins
Total Time: 1 hr

Servings per Recipe: 16
Calories 183 kcal
Fat 4.1 g
Carbohydrates 26.3g
Protein 10.9 g
Cholesterol 17 mg
Sodium 594 mg

Ingredients

- 1 lb ground beef
- 1 (20 oz.) can white or yellow hominy, rinsed and drained
- 2 (14.5 oz.) cans stewed tomatoes
- 1 (15.25 oz.) can whole kernel corn
- 1 (15 oz.) can kidney beans
- 2 (15 oz.) cans ranch-style beans
- 1 large yellow onion, diced
- 2 green chili peppers, diced

Directions

1. Stir fry your beef until it is fully done then remove the excess oils and place the meat in a big pot, add in: green chilies, hominy, onion, tomatoes, ranch beans, corn, and kidney beans.
2. Stir the mix then place a lid on the pot and cook the stew for 65 mins.
3. Enjoy.

Classical Beef Stew

🍲 Prep Time: 20 mins
🕐 Total Time: 2 hrs 20 mins

Servings per Recipe: 10
Calories   401 kcal
Fat   21.2 g
Carbohydrates   24.9 g
Protein   27.2 g
Cholesterol   79 mg
Sodium   436 mg

Ingredients

- 2 lbs cubed beef stew meat
- 3 tbsps vegetable oil
- 4 cubes beef bouillon, crumbled
- 4 C. water
- 1 tsp dried rosemary
- 1 tsp dried parsley
- 1/2 tsp ground black pepper
- 3 large potatoes, peeled and cubed
- 4 carrots, cut into 1 inch pieces
- 4 stalks celery, cut into 1 inch pieces
- 1 large onion, diced
- 2 tsps cornstarch
- 2 tsps cold water

Directions

1. Fry your beef in a big saucepan until it is brown. Combine your water and bouillon together until it is smooth, in a bowl, then add it with the beef. Stir the mix then combine in: pepper, parsley, and rosemary.
2. Get the mix boiling, set the heat to low, and let the contents cook for 65 mins.
3. Now add in onions, potatoes, celery and carrots. Add in 2 tsps of cold water and your cornstarch.
4. Stir the mix until everything is smooth then place a lid on the pot and let the mix cook for 60 more mins.
5. Enjoy.

COTTAGE CHEESE
Cinnamon Waffle

Prep Time: 10 mins
Total Time: 15 mins

Servings per Recipe: 3
Calories	254 kcal
Carbohydrates	23.2 g
Cholesterol	135 mg
Fat	8.5 g
Protein	20.8 g
Sodium	408 mg

Ingredients

- 1 C. old-fashioned oats
- 1 C. cottage cheese
- 2 eggs
- 3 egg whites
- 1 tsp honey
- 1 splash pure vanilla extract
- 1 pinch ground cinnamon

Directions

1. Heat your waffle cooker.
2. Get your blender, blend until smooth: cinnamon, oats, vanilla extract, egg whites, cottage cheese, and eggs
3. With a batch process: cook batter for 5 mins. Continue for remaining.
4. Enjoy.

Chicken Nugget Waffle

Prep Time: 15 mins
Total Time: 40 mins

Servings per Recipe: 6
Calories	489 kcal
Carbohydrates	40.6 g
Cholesterol	109 mg
Fat	27.5 g
Protein	19.7 g
Sodium	1155 mg

Ingredients

- 24 frozen chicken nuggets
- cooking spray
- 1 1/4 C. all-purpose flour
- 1/4 C. cornmeal
- 1 1/2 tsps white sugar
- 1 1/2 tsps baking powder
- 1 tsp salt
- 3/4 tsp baking soda
- 1/2 tsp ground black pepper
- 1/4 tsp cayenne pepper
- 1 3/4 C. buttermilk
- 1/3 C. vegetable oil
- 2 eggs, beaten

Directions

1. Set your oven to 400 degrees before doing anything else.
2. Cook your chicken nuggets for 15 mins. Until golden.
3. Heat your waffle cooker.
4. Get a bowl, sift evenly: Cayenne pepper, flour, black pepper, sugar, baking soda and salt.
5. Get a 2nd bowl, mix: eggs, buttermilk, and oil.
6. Combine both bowls to make batter. Evenly mix everything.
7. Coat your iron with nonstick spray.
8. In the middle of your iron put a piece of chicken. Take a tbsp of batter and coat the nugget. Cook for 5 mins. Repeat with all nuggets.
9. Enjoy warm.

COCONUT Waffle

 Prep Time: 15 mins
Total Time: 45 mins

Servings per Recipe: 8
Calories   303 kcal
Carbohydrates   25.1 g
Cholesterol   46 mg
Fat   20.8 g
Protein   7.2 g
Sodium   805 mg

Ingredients

2 C. spelt flour
1/4 C. flax seed meal
4 tsps baking powder
1 tbsp ground cinnamon
2 tsps baking soda
1 tsp Himalayan salt
1 3/4 C. coconut milk

1/4 C. coconut oil, melted
2 eggs, beaten
2 tbsps apple cider vinegar
1 tbsp vanilla extract

Directions

1. Get your waffle cooker hot.
2. Get a bowl, sift: salt, spelt flour, baking soda and powder, flax seed meal, and cinnamon.
3. Get a 2nd bowl, mix evenly: vanilla extract, coconut milk, vinegar, eggs, and coconut oil.
4. Mix both bowls evenly for make batter. Let it sit for 5 mins.
5. Coat your iron with nonstick spray.
6. Cook for 7 mins 1 C. of batter.
7. Enjoy warm.

Buttermilk Greek Waffle

Prep Time: 15 mins
Total Time: 35 mins

Servings per Recipe: 6
Calories	414 kcal
Carbohydrates	49.8 g
Cholesterol	107 mg
Fat	18.9 g
Protein	11.5 g
Sodium	839 mg

Ingredients

- 2 1/2 C. all-purpose flour
- 4 tsps baking powder
- 3/4 tsp salt
- 2 C. buttermilk
- 1/2 C. vanilla Greek-style yogurt
- 1/2 C. butter, melted
- 2 eggs, beaten
- 1 1/2 tbsps white sugar
- 3/4 C. chopped strawberries

Directions

1. Get your waffle maker hot.
2. Get a bowl, sift: salt, flour, and baking powder.
3. Get a 2nd bowl, evenly mix: sugar, buttermilk, eggs, Greek yogurt, butter, and strawberries.
4. Mix both bowls to make batter.
5. Coat waffle iron with nonstick spray. For 8 mins cook 1/3 C. of batter. Cook all the batter in this manner.
6. Enjoy.

Manufactured by Amazon.ca
Bolton, ON